Python 3 MCQ - Multiple Choice Questions n Answers for Tests, Quizzes - Python Students & Teachers

By S. C. Lewis

Version: 0.09

Multiple Choice Questions for Python 3

600 Plus MCQ's for Python Jobs, Tests & Quizzes

If you are learning Python programming on your own (whether you are learning from Python books, videos or online tutorials and lesson plans) this book is for you. These questions and answers can be used to test your knowledge of Python3. If you already know Python, you can still use it to check how many questions you can attempt on your own without any help. You may want to go through these questions before you appear for a job interview. If you are a teacher or tutor who is teaching Python, you'll find these MCQ useful as a tool to understand how much your students have learned what you have taught.

All these questions are based on **Python 3** and the target level of questions is Beginner Level - someone who is just starting to learn Python or someone who has recently learnt Python. Answer Key for these questions is provided at the end.

S.C. Lewis

FAQ

Q 1. These questions are based on which version of Python?
Ans: All the MCQ for this book are based on Python 3.

Q 2. The questions have been tested on which platforms?
Ans: These questions have been tested with Python 3.4.0 on Linux and Windows operating systems. You might want to download/update the newest Python version from www.Python.org for your own system before attempting these questions.

Q 3. I have just started to learn Python. Will I be able to answer these questions?
Ans: The questions for this book are written for beginners level and are intended for someone who has recently learnt Python. Someone who has just started to learn Python is likely to find these questions useful too. You might not be able to answer all the questions in first attempt but would be able to answer all if you keep coming back to these questions as you start becoming fluent in Python.

Q 4. When I run the statements given in the question, I am not able to get any of the 4 options as my output?
Ans: It is recommended that you try to run the statements for which some output is expected by saving them as a program in the IDLE File Editor only (unless noted otherwise) and if it not works as expected then only try it in IDLE shell (one statement at a time). Some statements work only in the File Editor while some work exclusively on the IDLE shell. In some rare cases, it might be because of the version of Python you are using and your operating system as some questions might give platform specific output.

Q 5. When I run the statements given in the question, the output is not in the same order or exactly same as the given answer?
Ans: This is because some statements and functions give a random output or an unsorted order of items. In such cases, you may select the answer which is most likely to be the possible answer based on your understanding of Python.

Q 6. What is the recommended approach to solve these questions?
Ans: The best approach to solve these questions is to take a pen(or pencil) & paper and try attempting these questions one by one.

S.C. Lewis

1. If you do not know the answer to a particular question (may be you have not learnt the topic yet), you may leave the answer for that question blank, skip that question for the moment and come back to attempt it after you have learnt that topic.

2. If you attempted a question but your answer was wrong, go through your Python notes (or books) again and then re-attempt that question later when you have thoroughly grasped that concept.

3. If you get all the answers right in your first attempt, Congratulations! you are doing something right. You can still come back to these questions after a while for revision and to keep those topics and the related concepts in your memory refreshed.

Q 7. Does the answer key contains the explanations to these questions too?

Ans: The answer key contains only the answers and does not contain the explanation to the answers. This is because most of the answers are self-explantory or very simple to understand if you have understood the basic concepts well. If you still face some difficulty, try thinking for a while and you'll know why. Or else, you might Google that statement or expression and you are likely to find your explanation easily but you might not need to go that far. If you still face any problems, feel free to let me know.

Python MCQ Topics

The topics on which these questions are based include:

Python basics
IDLE
user inputs
operations
arithmetic
assigning values
comparisons
writing statements
list
lists manipulation
tuple
set
dictionary
branching with if
while loop
for loop
functions
importing modules
built-in functions
built-in modules
working with strings
list comprehensions
file handling
reading and writing files
objects and classes

Python MCQ

1. Which of the following version of Python was released in December, 2015 by Python.org?

    a. 3.3
    b. 3.5.1
    c. 2.4
    d. 2.6

2. Python files are saved with the extension as ...?

    a. .python
    b. .pe
    c. .py
    d. .pi

3. What is the name of the GUI that comes in-built as an interactive shell with Python?

    a. PGUI
    b. Pyshell
    c. IDLE
    d. PythonSh

4. IDLE stands for ... ?

    a. Indigenous Development Lab
    b. Integrated Development Environment
    c. Integrated Developers Local Environment
    d. Indie Developers Environment

5. The function to display a specified message on the screen is ... ?

    a. print
    b. display
    c. run
    d. output

6. Which of the following is an assignment operator in Python?

    a. ==
    b. ===
    c. >>>
    d. =

7. Which of the following is used to initialize multiple variables with a common value?

    a. x = y: y = 33
    b. x = y = z = 33
    c. x = z; y = z; x = 33;

d. x & y & z = 33

8. Comments in Python begin with ...?

a. {
b. %
c. *
d. #

9. A user-specified value can be assigned to a variable with this function

a. user
b. enter
c. input
d. value

10. User input is read as ...?

a. Floating Decimal
b. Text String
c. Boolean Value
d. Integer

11. Output displayed by the print function will add this invisible character at the end of the line by default

a. \t
b. \n
c. \s
d. \r

12. Multiple values specified in parentheses to print function will display each value separated with this by default

a. Single Space
b. Double Space
c. A new Line
d. Double Lines

13. Which of the following will provide an ! character as alternative separator for the print function?

a. sep is !
b. separate = !
c. sep >> '!'
d. sep = '!'

14. Which of the following will provide a * character as alternative line ending for the print function?

a. end to *
b. end as *
c. end = '*'
d. ending = '*'

15.   For which type of error does the interpreter halts and reports the error but does not execute the program?

a. Semantic error
b. Syntax error
c. Runtime error
d. All type of errors

16.   For which type of error does the interpreter runs the program but halts at error and reports the error as an "Exception"?

a. Semantic error
b. Syntax error
c. Runtime error
d. All type of errors

17.   For which type of error does the interpreter runs the program and does not report an error?

a. Semantic error
b. Syntax error
c. Runtime error
d. All type of errors

18.   What will be the output after the following statements?

x = 6
y = 3
print(x / y)

a. 2.0
b. 2
c. 18
d. 18.0

19.   What will be the output after the following statements?

x = 8
y = 2
print(x // y)

a. 4.0
b. 4
c. 16
d. 16.0

20.   What will be the output after the following statements?

```
x = 5
y = 4
print(x % y)
```

a. 0
b. 20
c. 1.0
d. 1

21.   What will be the output after the following statements?

```
x = 3
y = 2
x += y
print(x)
```

a. 3
b. 2
c. 5
d. 1

22.   What will be the output after the following statements?

```
x = 5
y = 7
x *= y
print(x)
```

a. 7
b. 12
c. 5
d. 35

23.   What will be the output after the following statements?

```
x = 25
y = 15
x -= y
print(x)
```

a. 10
b. 25
c. 15
d. -15

24.   What will be the output after the following statements?

```
x = 30
```

```
y = 7
x %= y
print(x)
```

a. 4
b. 28
c. 2
d. 37

25.   What will be the output after the following statements?

```
x = 3
y = 7
print(x == y)
```

a. y = 7 and x = 3
b. True
c. x = 3 and y = 3
d. False

26.   What will be the output after the following statements?

```
x = 8
y = 6
print(x != y)
```

a. y = 6 and x = 8
b. True
c. x = 6 and y = 6
d. False

27.   What will be the output after the following statements?

```
x = 83
y = 57
print(x > y)
```

a. True
b. False
c. Yes
d. No

28.   What will be the output after the following statements?

```
x = 72
y = 64
print(x < y)
```

a. True
b. False

c. Yes
d. No

29. What will be the output after the following statements?

x = True
y = False
print(x and y)

a. True
b. False
c. Not defined
d. xy

30. What will be the output after the following statements?

x = True
y = False
print(x or y)

a. True
b. False
c. Not defined
d. xy

31. What will be the output after the following statements?

x = True
y = False
print(not x)

a. True
b. False
c. Not defined
d. y

32. What will be the output after the following statements?

x = True
y = False
print(not y)

a. True
b. False
c. Not defined
a. x

33. What will be the output after the following statements?

x = 20

```
y = 40
z = y if (y > x) else x
print(z)
```

a. True
b. False
c. 20
d. 40

34.   What will be the output after the following statements?

```
x = 50
y = 10
z = y if (y > x) else x
print(z)
```

a. True
b. False
c. 50
d. 10

35.   What will be the output after the following statements?

```
x = 65
y = 53
z = y if (x % 2 == 0) else x
print(z)
```

a. True
b. False
c. 65
d. 53

36.   What will be the output after the following statements?

```
x = 46
y = 98
z = y if (y % 2 == 0) else x
print(z)
```

a. True
b. False
c. 46
d. 98

37.   What will be the output after the following statements?

```
x = 2 * 4 + 7
print(x)
```

a. 30
b. 15
c. 22
d. 247

38.   What will be the output after the following statements?

x = 7 * (4 + 5)
print(x)

a. 63
b. 16
c. 33
d. 35

39.   What will be the output after the following statements?

x = '24' + '16'
print(x)

a. 40
b. 2416
c. 21
d. 46

40.   What will be the output after the following statements?

x = 15 + 35
print(x)

a. 40
b. 153
c. 50
d. 1535

41.   What will be the data type of x after the following statement if input entered is 18 ?

x = input('Enter a number: ')

a. Float
b. String
c. List
d. Integer

42.   What will be the data type of y after the following statements if input entered is 50?

x = input('Enter a number: ')
y = int(x)

a. Float

b. String
c. List
d. Integer

43. What will be the data type of y after the following statements?

x = 71
y = float(x)

a. Float
b. String
c. List
d. Integer

44. What will be the data type of y after the following statements?

x = 48
y = str(x)

a. Float
b. String
c. List
d. Integer

45. What will be the output after the following statements?

x = y = z = 8
print(y)

a. x
b. 8
c. z
d. y

46. What will be the value of x, y and z after the following statement?

x = y = z = 300

a. All three will have the value of 3
b. All three will have the value of 100
c. All three will have the value of 300
d. x and y will have arbitrary values, while z will have the value of 300

47. What will be the value of x, y and z after the following statement?

x, y, z = 3, 4, 5

a. All three will have the value of 3
b. All three will have the value of 345
c. x will have the value of 3, y will have the value 4 and z will have the value of 5

d. x and y will have arbitrary values, while z will have the value of 345

48. What is the data type of x after the following statement?

x = [7, 8, 9, 10]

a. List
b. Dictionary
c. Tuple
d. String

49. What is the data type of x after the following statement?

x = ['Today', 'Tomorrow', 'Yesterday']

a. List
b. Dictionary
c. Tuple
d. String

50. What will be the output after the following statements?

x = ['Today', 'Tomorrow', 'Yesterday']
y = x[1]
print(y)

a. x1
b. Today
c. Tomorrow
d. Yesterday

51. What will be the output after the following statements?

x = [25, 35, 45]
y = x[0]
print(y)

a. x0
b. 25
c. 35
d. 45

52. What will be the output after the following statements?

x = [10, 20, 30]
y = x[1] + x[2]
print(y)

a. 20
b. 30

c. 40
d. 50

53. What will be the output after the following statements?

```
x = ['Sunday', 'Monday', 'Tuesday']
y = x[1] + x[2]
print(y)
```

a. MondayTuesday
b. SundayMonday
c. SunMonday
d. Monday Tuesday

54. What will be the output after the following statements?

```
x = [[0.0, 1.0, 2.0],[4.0, 5.0, 6.0]]
y = x[1][2]
print(y)
```

a. 0.0
b. 1.0
c. 5.0
d. 6.0

55. What will be the output after the following statements?

```
x = [[0.0, 1.0, 2.0],[4.0, 5.0, 6.0]]
y = x[0][1] + x[1][0]
print(y)
```

a. 1.0
b. 4.0
c. 5.0
d. 6.0

56. What will be the output after the following statements?

```
x = 3
y = 4
print(x*y)
```

a. 3
b. 4
c. 3 4
d. 12

57. What will be the output after the following statements?

```
x = [15, 45, 85, 95]
```

print(x[3]-x[1])

a. 30
b. 40
c. 50
d. 10

58.   What will be the output after the following statements?

x = [5, 4, 3, 2]
print(x)

a. [5, 4, 3, 2]
b. 5, 4, 3, 2
c. 5432
d. (5, 4, 3, 2)

59.   What will be the output after the following statements?

x = [5, 4, 3, 2]
x.append(1)
print(x)

a. [5, 4, 3, 2]
b. 5, 4, 3, 2, 1
c. 5432
d. [5, 4, 3, 2, 1]

60.   What will be the output after the following statements?

x = [5, 4, 3, 2]
x.insert(1, 0)
print(x)

a. [5, 1, 3, 2, 0]
b. [5, 0, 4, 3, 2]
c. [0, 5, 4, 3, 2]
d. [1, 5, 4, 3, 2]

61.   What will be the output after the following statements?

x = [5, 4, 3, 2]
x.remove(2)
print(x)

a. [5, 3, 2]
b. [5, 4, 3]
c. [5, 4, 2]
d. [3, 2]

62. What will be the output after the following statements?

```
x = [5, 4, 3, 2, 1]
print(x.pop(3))
```

a. 4
b. 3
c. 2
d. 1

63. What will be the output after the following statements?

```
x = [5, 4, 3, 2, 1]
print(x.index(1))
```

a. 4
b. 3
c. 2
d. 1

64. What will be the output after the following statements?

```
x = [5, 4, 3, 2, 1]
x.extend(x)
print(x)
```

a. [5, 4, 3, 2, 1]
b. []
c. [1, 2, 3, 4, 5]
d. [5, 4, 3, 2, 1, 5, 4, 3, 2, 1]

65. What will be the output after the following statements?

```
x = [5, 4, 3, 2, 1]
y = [0, 5, 10]
x.extend(y)
print(x)
```

a. [5, 4, 3, 2, 1, 0, 5, 10]
b. []
c. [5, 4, 3, 2, 1]
d. [0, 5, 10, 5, 4, 3, 2, 1]

66. What will be the output after the following statements?

```
x = [5, 4, 3, 2, 1]
y = [10, 5, 0]
x.extend(y)
print(y)
```

a. [5, 4, 3, 2, 1, 10, 5, 0]
b. []
c. [10, 5, 0, 5, 4, 3, 2, 1]
d. [10, 5, 0]

67.   What will be the output after the following statements?

```
x = [5, 4, 3, 2, 1]
y = [10, 5, 0]
y.extend(x)
print(y)
```

a. [5, 4, 3, 2, 1, 10, 5, 0]
b. [10, 5, 0, 5, 4, 3, 2, 1]
c. [5, 4, 3, 2, 1]
d. [10, 5, 0]

68.   What will be the output after the following statements?

```
x = [5, 4, 3, 2, 1]
x.reverse()
print(x)
```

a. [0, 1, 2, 3, 4, 5]
b. [0, 5, 4, 3, 2, 1]
c. [5, 4, 3, 2, 1, 0]
d. [1, 2, 3, 4, 5]

69.   What will be the output after the following statements?

```
x = [25, 14, 53, 62, 11]
x.sort()
print(x)
```

a. [11, 14, 25, 53, 62]
b. [25, 14, 53, 62, 11]
c. [62, 53, 25, 14, 11]
d. [25, 53, 62, 14, 11]

70.   What will be the output after the following statements?

```
x = ['25', 'Today', '53', 'Sunday', '15']
x.sort()
print(x)
```

a. ['Today', 'Sunday', '15', '25', '53']
b. ['Sunday', 'Today', '15', '25', '53']
c. ['15', '25', '53', 'Sunday', 'Today']
d. ['15', '25', '53', 'Today', 'Sunday']

71. What will be the output after the following statements?

```
x = [25, 'Today', 53, 'Sunday', 15]
x.reverse()
print(x)
```

a. ['Today', 'Sunday', 15, 25, 53]
b. [15, 'Sunday', 53, 'Today', 25]
c. [15, 25, 53, 'Sunday', 'Today']
d. [15, 25, 53, 'Today', 'Sunday']

72. What will be the output after the following statements?

```
x = [25, 35, 53, 25, 52, 35, 25]
print(x.count(25))
```

a. 25
b. 3
c. 53
d. 35

73. What will be the output after the following statements?

```
x = [25, 35, 53, 25, 52, 35, 25]
print(len(x))
```

a. 25
b. 5
c. 7
d. 35

74. What will be the output after the following statements?

```
x = [25, 35, 53, 25, 52, 35, 25]
len(x)
print(x)
```

a. 25
b. 5
c. 7
d. [25, 35, 53, 25, 52, 35, 25]

75. What will be the output after the following statements?

```
x = [25, 35, 53, 25, 52, 35, 25]
del x[3]
print(x)
```

a. [25, 35, 53, 52, 35, 25]
b. [25, 5, 5, 25, 52, 5, 25]

c. [35, 53, 52, 35]
d. [25, 35, 53, 25, 52, 35, 25]

76.   What will be the output after the following statements?

```
x = [5, 3, 6, 2, 4, 0, 1]
del x[2:3]
print(x)
```

a. [5, 3, 6, 4, 0, 1]
b. [5, 3, 2, 4, 0, 1]
c. [5, 6, 2, 4, 0, 1]
d. [5, 4, 0, 1]

77.   What will be the output after the following statements?

```
x = [5, 3, 6, 2, 4, 0, 7]
del x[0:7]
print(x)
```

a. []
b. [5, 3, 6, 2, 4, 0, 7]
c. [5, 3, 6, 2, 4, 0]
d. [3, 6, 2, 4, 0]

78.   What will be the output after the following statements?

```
x = [5, 3, 6, 2, 4, 0, 7]
del x[0:4]
print(x)
```

a. []
b. [5, 3, 6, 2, 7]
c. [5, 3, 6, 2, 4, 0]
d. [4, 0, 7]

79.   What will be the output after the following statements?

```
x = [5, 3, 6, 2, 4, 0, 7]
del x[:]
print(x)
```

a. []
b. [5, 3, 6, 2, 7]
c. [5, 3, 6, 2, 4, 0]
d. [4, 0, 7]

80.   What will be the output after the following statements?

```
x = [4, 0, 7]
```

```
y = str(x[0]) + str(x[1])
print(y)
```

a. 11
b. 4
c. 40
d. 7

81.   What will be the output after the following statements?

```
x = [4, 0, 7]
y = float(x[0] + x[2])
print(y)
```

a. 11
b. 11.0
c. 47.0
d. 47

82.   What will be the data type of x after the following statement?

```
x = (34, 81, 50)
```

a. List
b. String
c. Dictionary
d. Tuple

83.   What will be the data type of x after the following statement?

```
x = 'Python 3 Test'
```

a. List
b. String
c. Dictionary
d. Tuple

84.   What will be the data type of x after the following statement?

```
x = [2290, 376, 198]
```

a. List
b. String
c. Dictionary
d. Tuple

85.   What will be the data type of x after the following statement?

```
x = {'lang' :'Python', 'version' : '3'}
```

a. List
b. Set
c. Dictionary
d. Tuple

86.   What will be the data type of x after the following statement?

x = {2015, 2016, 2017, 2018}

a. List
b. Set
c. Dictionary
d. Tuple

87.   What will be the data type of x after the following statement?

x = [2016, 'Leap Year', 'True']

a. List
b. String
c. Dictionary
d. Boolean

88.   What will be the data type of x after the following statement?

x = False

a. List
b. String
c. Dictionary
d. Boolean

89.   Which of the following function can be used to find the data type of a variable?

a. data()
b. type()
c. true()
d. str()

90.   What will be the output after the following statements?

x = [24, 50, 37]
y = 24 in x
print(y)

a. x[0]
b. [24]
c. True
d. False

91. What will be the output after the following statements?

```
x = {'A', 'B', 'C'}
y = 'b' in x
print(y)
```

a. x[1]
b. ['B']
c. True
d. False

92. What will be the output after the following statements?

```
x = 'Python'
y = 'y' in x
print(y)
```

a. [1]
b. y
c. True
d. False

93. What will be the output after the following statements?

```
x = {0:4, 1:8, 2:16, 3:32}
y = 0 in x
print(y)
```

a. x[0]
b. [24]
c. True
d. False

94. What will be the output after the following statements?

```
x = {0:4, 1:8, 2:16, 3:32}
y = 8 in x
print(y)
```

a. x[0]
b. [24]
c. True
d. False

95. What will be the data type of x after the following statements?

```
false = "This is not true"
x = false
```

a. List

b. String
c. Dictionary
d. Boolean

96.   Which of the following is immutable (values that cannot be changed)?

a. List
b. Dictionary
c. Tuple
d. Set

97.   Which of the following has only unique values?

a. List
b. Dictionary
c. Tuple
d. Set

98.   What will be the output after the following statements?

```
x = {0:4, 1:8, 2:16, 3:32}
print(x.keys())
```

a. [0, 1, 2, 3]
b. {0, 1, 2, 3}
c. (0, 1, 2, 3)
d. 0, 1, 2, 3

99.   What will be the output after the following statements?

```
x = {0:4, 1:8, 2:16, 3:32}
print(x.values())
```

a. [4, 8, 16, 32]
b. {4, 8, 16, 32}
c. (4, 8, 16, 32)
d. 4, 8, 16, 32

100.   What will be the output after the following statements?

```
x = {1:'Jan', 2:'Feb', 3:'March', 4:'April'}
print(x[2])
```

a. Jan
b. Feb
c. March
d. April

101.   What will be the output after the following statements?

```
x = {0:4, 1:8, 2:16, 3:32}
print(list(x.values())[2])
```

a. [4, 8]
b. [4, 8, 16]
c. 16
d. 8

102.   What will be the output after the following statements?

```
x = {0:4, 1:8, 2:16, 3:32}
print(x.items())
```

a. (4, 8, 16, 32)
b. [4, 8, 16, 32]
c. [0, 1, 2, 3]
d. [(0, 4), (1, 8), (2, 16), (3, 32)]

103.   What will be the output after the following statements?

```
x = {5:4, 8:8, 3:16, 9:32}
print(sorted(x.items()))
```

a. [4, 8, 16, 32]
b. [(3, 16), (5, 4), (8, 8), (9, 32)]
c. [3, 5, 8, 9]
d. [(4, 5), (8, 8), (16, 3), (32, 9)]

104.   What will be the output after the following statements?

```
x = 7
if x > 5:
      print(20)
```

a. 20
b. 5
c. x
d. 7

105.   What will be the output after the following statements?

```
x = 8
if x > 8:
      print(20)
else:
      print(10)
```

a. 20
b. x
c. 10

```
```

d. 8

106.   What will be the output after the following statements?

```
x = 40
if x > 10:
      print(20)
elif x == 40:
      print(10)
else:
      print(30)
```

a. 20
b. 40
c. 10
d. 30

107.   What will be the output after the following statements?

```
x = 15
if x > 15:
      print(0)
elif x == 15:
      print(1)
else:
      print(2)
```

a. 0
b. 1
c. 2
d. 15

108.   What will be the output after the following statements?

```
x = 5
if x > 15:
      print('yes')
elif x == 15:
      print('equal')
else:
      print('no')
```

a. 15
b. yes
c. equal
d. no

109.   What will be the output after the following statements?

```
x = 50
```

```
if x > 10  and x < 15:
    print('true')
elif x > 15  and x < 25:
    print('not true')
elif x > 25  and x < 35:
    print('false')
else:
    print('not false')
```

a. true
b. false
c. not true
d. not false

110.   What will be the output after the following statements?

```
x = 25
if x > 10  and x < 15:
    print('true')
elif x > 15  and x < 25:
    print('not true')
elif x > 25  and x < 35:
    print('false')
else:
    print('not false')
```

a. true
b. false
c. not true
d. not false

111.   What will be the output after the following statements?

```
x = 15
if x > 10  and x <= 15:
    print('true')
elif x > 15  and x < 25:
    print('not true')
elif x > 25  and x < 35:
    print('false')
else:
    print('not false')
```

a. true
b. false
c. not true
d. not false

112.   What will be the output after the following statements?

```
x = 25
if x > 10  and x <= 15:
    print('true')
elif x >= 15  and x < 25:
    print('not true')
elif x >= 25  and x < 35:
    print('false')
else:
    print('not false')
```

a. true
b. false
c. not true
d. not false

113.   What will be the output after the following statements?

```
x = 25
if x >= 10  and x <= 15:
    print('true')
elif x >= 15  and x <= 25:
    print('not true')
elif x >= 25  and x <= 35:
    print('false')
else:
    print('not false')
```

a. true
b. false
c. not true
d. not false

114.   What will be the output after the following statements?

```
x = 20
if x <= 10 or x >= 75:
    print('true')
elif x <= 15 or x >= 55:
    print('not true')
elif x <= 25 or x >= 35:
    print('false')
else:
    print('not false')
```

a. true
b. false
c. not true
d. not false

115.   What will be the output after the following statements?

```
x = 30
if x <= 10 or x >= 75:
    print('true')
elif x <= 15 or x >= 55:
    print('not true')
elif x <= 25 or x >= 35:
    print('false')
else:
    print('not false')
```

a. true
b. false
c. not true
d. not false

116.   What will be the output after the following statements?

```
x = 80
if x <= 10 or x >= 75:
    print('true')
elif x <= 15 or x >= 55:
    print('not true')
elif x <= 25 or x >= 35:
    print('false')
else:
    print('not false')
```

a. true
b. false
c. not true
d. not false

117.   What will be the output after the following statements?

```
x = 60
if x <= 10 or x >= 75:
    print('true')
elif x <= 15 or x >= 55:
    print('not true')
elif x <= 25 or x >= 35:
    print('false')
else:
    print('not false')
```

a. true
b. false
c. not true
d. not false

118. What will be the output after the following statements?

```
x = 68
if x <= 50 and x >= 25:
    print('true')
elif x <= 60 or x >= 55:
    print('not true')
elif x <= 70 and x >= 35:
    print('false')
else:
    print('not false')
```

a. true
b. false
c. not true
d. not false

119. What will be the output after the following statements?

```
x = 99
if x <= 30 or x >= 100:
    print('true')
elif x >= 50 and x <= 80:
    print('not true')
elif x >= 100 or x <= 75:
    print('false')
else:
    print('not false')
```

a. true
b. false
c. not true
d. not false

120. What will be the output after the following statements?

```
x = 70
if x <= 30 or x >= 100:
    print('true')
elif x <= 50 and x == 50:
    print('not true')
elif x >= 150 or x <= 75:
    print('false')
else:
    print('not false')
```

a. true
b. false
c. not true
d. not false

121. What will be the output after the following statements?

```
x = 40
y = 25
if x + y >= 100:
    print('true')
elif x + y == 50:
    print('not true')
elif x + y <= 90:
    print('false')
else:
    print('not false')
```

a. true
b. false
c. not true
d. not false

122. What will be the output after the following statements?

```
x = 1
while x < 10:
    print(x, end='')
    x = x + 1
```

a. 123456789
b. 1
c. 10
d. 2

123. What will be the output after the following statements?

```
x = 0
while x < 10:
    print(x, end='')
    x += 4
```

a. 0123456789
b. 123456789
c. 4123456789
d. 048

124. What will be the output after the following statements?

```
x = 0
y = 4
while x + y < 10:
    print(x, end='')
    x += 1
```

a. 012345
b. 0123456789
c. 4123456789
d. 048

125.   What will be the output after the following statements?

```
x = 0
y = 4
while x + y < 10:
    x += 1
    print(x, end='')
```

a. 012345
b. 0123456
c. 123456
d. 0123456

126.   What will be the output after the following statements?

```
x = 1
y = 4
while x * y < 10:
    print(y, end='')
    y += 1
```

a. 012345
b. 456789
c. 123456789
d. 0123456789

127.   What will be the output after the following statements?

```
x = 1
y = 4
while x * y < 10:
    print(y, end='')
    x += 1
    y += 1
```

a. 4
b. 48
c. 148
d. 0123456789

128.   What will be the output after the following statements?

```
x = 1
y = 4
```

```
while x * y <= 10:
    print(x, end=")
    x += 1
    y += 1
```

a. 4
b. 48
c. 14
d. 12

129.   What will be the output after the following statements?

```
x, y = 2, 5
while y - x < 5:
    print(x*y, end=' ')
    x += 3
    y += 4
```

a. 1045
b. 10 45
c. 34
d. 3 4 10 45

130.   What will be the output after the following statements?

```
x, y = 0, 1
while y < 10:
    print(y, end=' ')
    x, y = y, x + y
```

a. 1 1 2 3 5 8
b. 112358
c. 0123456789
d. 0 2 4 6 8

131.   What will be the output after the following statements?

```
x = 1
while x < 4:
    x += 1
    y = 1
    while y < 3:
        print(y, end=' ')
        y += 1
```

a. 1 1 2 2
b. 1 1 2 2 3 3 4 4
c. 1 2 3 4
d. 1 2 1 2 1 2

132. What will be the output after the following statements?

```
x = y = 1
while x < 4:
    x += 1
    while y < 3:
        print(y, end=' ')
        y += 1
```

a. 1 1 2 2
b. 1 2
c. 1 2 3 4
d. 1 2 1 2 1 2

133. What type of loop is this?

```
x = 1
while x < 5:
    print(x, end='')
```

a. Closed loop
b. One time loop
c. Infinite loop
d. Evergreen loop

134. What will be the output after the following statements?

```
x = 'hello'
for i in x:
    print(i, end='')
```

a. h
b. hello
c. h e l l o
d. i x

135. What will be the output after the following statements?

```
for i in range(5):
    print(i, end='')
```

a. 5
b. 1 5
c. 012345
d. 01234

136. What will be the output after the following statements?

```
for i in range(1,5):
    print(i, end='')
```

a. 15
b. 12345
c. 1234
d. 012345

137.   What will be the output after the following statements?

```
for i in range(1,25,5):
    print(i, end=' ')
```

a. 1 6 11 16 21
b. 1 5 10 15 20 25
c. 1 5 25
d. 16111621

138.   What will be the output after the following statements?

```
x = ['P', 'y', 't', 'h', 'o', 'n']
for i in x:
    print(i, end='')
```

a. P
b. python
c. Pytho
d. Python

139.   What will be the output after the following statements?

```
x = ('a', 'b', 'c', 'd')
for i in x:
    print(i, end=' ')
```

a. abcd
b. a b c d
c. False
d. True

140.   What will be the output after the following statements?

```
x = {'x', 'z', 'y'}
for i in x:
    print(i, end='')
```

a. x z y
b. xzy
c. False
d. True

141.   What will be the output after the following statements?

```
x = {'z:1', 'y:2', 'x:3'}
for i in x:
    print(i, end=' ')
```

a. x y z
b. 1 2 3
c. x:3 y:2 z:1
d. True

142.   What will be the output after the following statements?

```
x = ['P', 'y', 't', 'h', 'o', 'n']
for i in enumerate(x):
    print(i, end='')
```

a. ('P')('y')('t')('h')('o')('n')
b. python
c. python
d. (0, 'P')(1, 'y')(2, 't')(3, 'h')(4, 'o')(5, 'n')

143.   What will be the output after the following statements?

```
x = {'x':1, 'y':2, 'z':3}
for i in x:
    print(i, end=' ')
```

a. x y z
b. 1 2 3
c. x:1 y:2 z:3
d. True

144.   What will be the output after the following statements?

```
x = {'x':1, 'y':2, 'z':3}
for i, j in x.items():
    print(i, j, end=' ')
```

a. x y z
b. x 1 y 2 z 3
c. x:1 y:2 z:3
d. x, 1, y, 2, z, 3

145.   What will be the output after the following statements?

```
x = ['p', 'y', 't', 'h', 'o', 'n']
y = ['0', '1', '2', '3', '4', '5']
for i in zip(x, y):
    print(i, end='')
```

a. ('P')('y')('t')('h')('o')('n')
b. python 0 1 2 3 4 5
c. ('p', '0')('y', '1')('t', '2')('h', '3')('o', '4')('n', '5')
d. (0, 'P')(1, 'y')(2, 't')(3, 'h')(4, 'o')(5, 'n')

146.   What will be the output after the following statements?

```
for i in range(1,5):
    print(i, end='')
    if i == 3:
        break
```

a. 123
b. 1234
c. 12
d. 12345

147.   What will be the output after the following statements?

```
for i in range(0,5):
    if i == 2:
        break
    print(i, end='')
```

a. 12
b. 01
c. 012
d. 0123

148.   What will be the output after the following statements?

```
for i in range(1,5):
    if i == 3:
        continue
    print(i, end=' ')
```

a. 1 2 4
b. 1 2 3 4
c. 1 2
d. 1 2 3

149.   What will be the output after the following statements?

```
for i in range(0,5):
    print(i, end='')
    if i == 2:
        continue
```

a. 0124
b. 01234

c. 12
d. 1345

150.   What will be the output after the following statements?

```
myvar = 5
def printvar() :
     print(myvar)
printvar()
```

a. 01245
b. 12345
c. 5
d. 1234

151.   What is printvar in the following statements?

```
myvar = 5
def printvar() :
     print(myvar)
printvar()
```

a. A list
b. A string
c. An integer
d. A function

152.   What will be the output after the following statements?

```
myvar = 5
def printvar() :
     print(myvar, end =")
printvar()
printvar()
```

a. 55
b. 5 5
c. 5
d. 10

153.   What will be the output after the following statements?

```
def call(var) :
     print(var, end =")
call(45)
```

a. 55
b. 4 5
c. 45
d. var

154.   What will be the output after the following statements?

```
def call(var1, var2) :
    print(var1 + var2, end =")
call(10, 40)
```

a. 10
b. 50
c. 40
d. 10 + 40

155.   What will be the output after the following statements?

```
def call(var1, var2, var3) :
    print(var1 * var2 * var3, end =")
a = b = c = 10
call(a, b, c)
```

a. 1000
b. 10
c. 30
d. 10 * 10 * 10

156.   What will be the output after the following statements?

```
def call(var1=20, var2=5, var3=2) :
    print(var1 * var2 * var3, end =")
call()
```

a. 100
b. 1000
c. 2052
d. 200

157.   What will be the output after the following statements?

```
def call(var1=20, var2=5, var3=2) :
    print(var1 * var2 * var3, end =")
call(5,9,7)
```

a. 597
b. 315
c. 2052
d. 200

158.   What will be the output after the following statements?

```
def call(var1=20, var2=5, var3=2) :
    print(var1 * var2 * var3, end =")
```

call(5,7)

a. 57
b. 315
c. 70
d. 200

159.   What will be the output after the following statements?

```
def call(var1=20, var2=5, var3=2) :
     print((var1 * var2) - var3, end ='')
call(var2=5, var3=3, var1=4)
```

a. 17
b. 98
c. 70
d. 11

160.   What will be the output after the following statements?

```
def call(var1=20, var2=5, var3=2) :
     print((var1 * var2) - var3, end ='')
call(7,4)
```

a. 17
b. 98
c. 26
d. 11

161.   What will be the output after the following statements?

```
def call(x, y) :
     return x * y
print(call(5, 3))
```

a. 18
b. 5, 3
c. 15
d. 8

162.   What will be the output after the following statements?

```
def call(y, x) :
   return x / y
z = call(4, 9)
print(z)
```

a. 0.444445
b. 2
c. 0

d. 2.25

163.   What will be the output after the following statements?

```
def call(x,y) :
   if y == 0:
      return
   return y - x
print(call(8,2))
```

a. 6
b. -6
c. 2
d. 6.0

164.   What will be the output after the following statements?

```
def call(x,y) :
   if x == 0:
      return
   return y + x
print(call(0,5))
```

a. 5
b. 5.0
c. 0
d. None

165.   What will be the output after the following statements?

```
y = lambda x: x*4
print(y(6))
```

a. 24
b. 24.0
c. 6: 24
d. 36

166.   What will be the output after the following statements?

```
x = 27
if x < 25:
   print(x)
else:
   pass
```

a. None
b. 25
c. 27
d. No output

167.   Which of the following is not a core data structure in Python?

a. List
b. Module
c. Dictionary
d. Tuple

168.   What will be the output after the following statements?

```
def gen():
   x = 0
   while True:
     yield x
     x += 1
y = gen()
print(next(y), end='')
print(next(y), end='')
print(next(y), end='')
```

a. 012
b. 123
c. 111
d. 000

169.   What will be the output after the following statements?

```
def gen():
   x = 2
   while True:
     yield x
     x += 1
y = gen()
for i in y:
   if i >= 5:
     break
   else:
     print(i, end='')
```

a. 0123
b. 123
c. 12345
d. 234

170.   What do you type to enter the interactive help mode of Python?

a. HELP
b. save
c. help()
d. help

171.   What does the following statement do?

import random

a. Imports the random module
b. Imports a random module from a list of modules
c. Imports the random function
d. imports the directory named random

172.   What does the following statement do?

import keyword, sys

a. Imports all the python keywords
b. Imports the keyword and sys modules
c. Imports the keyword and sys functions
d. imports the directories named keyword and sys

173.   What will be the output after the following statements?

import random as rd
print(rd.randint(4,7))

a. A random float value between 4 and 7, including 4 and 7
b. A random float value between 4 and 7, excluding 4 and 7
c. A random integer value between 4 and 7, excluding 4 and 7
d. A random integer value between 4 and 7, including 4 and 7

174.   What will be the output after the following statements?

import random as rd
print(rd.random())

a. A random float value between 0 and 1
b. A random integer value between 0 and 1
c. A random float value between 0 and 10
d. A random integer value between 0 and 10

175.   What will be the output after the following statements?

from random import *
x = [0, 2, 4, 6, 8, 10]
print(sample(x, 3))

a. A dictionary containing 3 random keys from list x
b. Three random integer values between 0 and 10
c. A list containing 3 random elements from list x
d. A tuple containing 2 random elements from list x

176. Which of the following can be a possible output after the following statements?

from random import *
print(sample(range(0,10), 3))

a. [4, 11, 30]
b. [3, 15, 10]
c. [1, 5, 7, 4]
d. [1, 5, 0]

177. What does the following statements do?

import sys
print(sys.version)

a. Displays the Python version
b. Displays the operating system version
c. Displays the date
d. Displays the year

178. What does the following statements do?

import sys
print(sys.executable)

a. Displays the Python version
b. Displays the operating system version
c. Displays the location of the Python interpreter
d. Displays the date and time

179. What does the following statements do?

import keyword
print(keyword.kwlist)

a. Displays the list of Python modules
b. Displays a list of all the Python keywords
c. Displays a random keyword from the Python keywords
d. Displays the date and time

180. What will be the output after the following statements?

import math
print(math.floor(67.3))

a. 67
b. 68
c. 67.0
d. 68.0

181. What will be the output after the following statements?

```
import math
print(math.ceil(21.4))
```

a. 21
b. 22
c. 21.0
d. 22.0

182. What will be the output after the following statements?

```
import math
print(math.sqrt(4))
```

a. 2.1
b. 2
c. 2.0
d. 4.0

183. What will be the output after the following statements?

```
import math
print(math.pow(3,2))
```

a. 6
b. 9
c. 6.0
d. 9.0

184. What does the following statements do?

```
import datetime
print(datetime.datetime.today())
```

a. Displays current date and time
b. Displays a list of all the hours remaining till midnight
c. Displays a random time from today's date
d. Displays today's weekday name

185. What does the following statements do?

```
from datetime import *
print(getattr(datetime.today(),'hour'))
```

a. Displays current date and time
b. Displays a list of all the hours remaining till midnight
c. Displays current hour of the day
d. Displays the number of hours in a day

186.   What does the following statements do?

```
from datetime import *
print(getattr(datetime.today(),'year'))
```

a. Displays current date and year
b. Displays current year
c. Displays the number of months in a year
d. Displays the number of days in a year

187.   What does the following statements do?

```
from datetime import *
print(datetime.today().strftime('%A'))
```

a. Displays the full month name
b. Displays the abbreviated month name
c. Displays the abbreviated day name
d. Displays the full weekday name

188.   What does the following statements do?

```
from datetime import *
print(datetime.today().strftime('%B'))
```

a. Displays the full weekday name
b. Displays the full month name
c. Displays the abbreviated day name
d. Displays the abbreviated month name

189.   What does the following statements do?

```
from datetime import *
print(datetime.today().strftime('%d'))
```

a. Displays the hour number of 12-hour clock
b. Displays the date and time appropriate for locale
c. Displays the day of the month number (from 01 to 31)
d. Displays the microsecond number (from 0 to 999999)

190.   What does the following statements do?

```
from datetime import *
print(datetime.today().strftime('%c'))
```

a. Displays the date and time appropriate for locale
b. Displays the microsecond number (from 0 to 999999)
c. Displays the hour number of 12-hour clock
d. Displays the hour number of 24-hour clock

191. What does the following statements do?

from datetime import *
print(datetime.today().strftime('%f'))

a. Displays the date and time appropriate for locale
b. Displays the microsecond number (from 0 to 999999)
c. Displays the hour number of 24-hour clock
d. Displays the hour number of 12-hour clock

192. What does the following statements do?

from datetime import *
print(datetime.today().strftime('%I'))

a. Displays the hour number of 12-hour clock
b. Displays the minute number from 00 to 59
c. Displays the hour number of 24-hour clock
d. Displays the day number of the year from 000 to 366

193. What does the following statements do?

from datetime import *
print(datetime.today().strftime('%H'))

a. Displays the minute number from 00 to 59
b. Displays the hour number of 12-hour clock
c. Displays the hour number of 24-hour clock
d. Displays the day number of the year from 000 to 366

194. What does the following statements do?

from datetime import *
print(datetime.today().strftime('%j'))

a. Displays the month number from 01 to 12
b. Displays the minute number from 00 to 59
c. Displays the day number of the year from 000 to 366
d. Displays the second number from 00 to 59

195. What does the following statements do?

from datetime import *
print(datetime.today().strftime('%M'))

a. Displays the month number from 01 to 12
b. Displays the second number from 00 to 59
c. Displays the AM or PM equivalent for locale
d. Displays the minute number from 00 to 59

196.   What does the following statements do?

from datetime import *
print(datetime.today().strftime('%m'))

a. Displays the minute number from 00 to 59
b. Displays the month number from 01 to 12
c. Displays the second number from 00 to 59
d. Displays the AM or PM equivalent for locale

197.   What does the following statements do?

from datetime import *
print(datetime.today().strftime('%p'))

a. Displays the AM or PM equivalent for locale
b. Displays the minute number from 00 to 59
c. Displays the month number from 01 to 12
d. Displays the second number from 00 to 59

198.   What does the following statements do?

from datetime import *
print(datetime.today().strftime('%S'))

a. Displays the AM or PM equivalent for locale
b. Displays the second number from 00 to 59
c. Displays the week number of the year from 00 to 53
d. Displays the month number from 01 to 12

199.   What does the following statements do?

from datetime import *
print(datetime.today().strftime('%W'))

a. Displays the weekday number from 0(Sunday) to 6(Saturday)
b. Displays the AM or PM equivalent for locale
c. Displays the date appropriate for locale
d. Displays the week number of the year from 00 to 53

200.   What does the following statements do?

from datetime import *
print(datetime.today().strftime('%w'))

a. Displays the week number of the year from 00 to 53
b. Displays the date appropriate for locale
c. Displays the weekday number from 0(Sunday) to 6(Saturday)
d. Displays the time appropriate for locale

201.   What does the following statements do?

```
from datetime import *
print(datetime.today().strftime('%x'))
```

a. Displays the time appropriate for locale
b. Displays the current year as 00 to 99
c. Displays the current year as 0001 to 9999
d. Displays the date appropriate for locale

202.   What does the following statements do?

```
from datetime import *
print(datetime.today().strftime('%X'))
```

a. Displays the current year as 0001 to 9999
b. Displays the timezone name
c. Displays the time appropriate for locale
d. Displays the current year as 00 to 99

203.   What does the following statements do?

```
from datetime import *
print(datetime.today().strftime('%y'))
```

a. Displays the current year as 00 to 99
b. Displays the current year as 0001 to 9999
c. Displays the timezone name
d. Displays the timezone offset from UTC as +HHMM or -HHMM

204.   What does the following statements do?

```
from datetime import *
print(datetime.today().strftime('%Y'))
```

a. Displays the current year as 0001 to 9999
b. Displays the timezone name
c. Displays the timezone offset from UTC as +HHMM or -HHMM
d. Displays the full month name

205.   What does the following statements do?

```
from datetime import *
print(datetime.today().strftime('%Z'))
```

a. Displays the timezone offset from UTC as +HHMM or -HHMM
b. Displays the timezone name
c. Displays the abbreviated month name
d. Displays the full month name

206.   What does the following statements do?

from datetime import *
print(datetime.today().strftime('%z'))

a. Displays the full month name
b. Displays the abbreviated month name
c. Displays the abbreviated day name
d. Displays the timezone offset from UTC as +HHMM or -HHMM

207.   What does the following statements do?

from datetime import *
print(datetime.today().strftime('%a'))

a. Displays the full month name
b. Displays the full day name
c. Displays the abbreviated day name
d. Displays the abbreviated month name

208.   What does the following statements do?

from datetime import *
print(datetime.today().strftime('%b'))

a. Displays the full month name
b. Displays the abbreviated month name
c. Displays the full day name
d. Displays the abbreviated day name

209.   What does the following statements do?

from time import *
print(time())

a. Displays the current time in seconds since the Epoch as a floating point number
b. Displays the current time in minutes since the Epoch as a floating point number
c. Displays the current time in seconds since the Epoch as an integer
d. Displays the current time in minutes since the Epoch as an integer

210.   What does the following statements do?

from time import *
sleep(3)

a. Pauses the execution of the program by 3 minutes
b. Pauses the execution of the program by 3 seconds
c. Displays the current time in seconds since the Epoch as an integer
d. Displays the current time in minutes since the Epoch as an integer

211. What will be the output after the following statements?

```
x = 'Python'
y = 'MCQ'
print(x + y)
```

a. Python Python
b. MCQ MCQ
c. Python MCQ
d. PythonMCQ

212. What will be the output after the following statements?

```
x = 'Python '
print(x*3)
```

a. Pyt Pyt Pyt
b. t
c. Python Python Python
d. PythonPythonPython

213. What will be the output after the following statements?

```
x = 'Python '
print(x[4])
```

a. h
b. t
c. Python Python Python Python
d. o

214. What will be the output after the following statements?

```
x = 'Python'
print(x[2:4])
```

a. Pyth
b. th
c. tho
d. thon

215. What will be the output after the following statements?

```
x = 'Python'
print(x[:])
```

a. yth
b. Pn
c. Python
d. PythonPythonPython

216.   What will be the output after the following statements?

```
x = 'Python'
print('y' in x)
```

a. y
b. Y
c. Python
d. True

217.   What will be the output after the following statements?

```
x = 'Python'
print('p' not in x)
```

a. p
b. P
c. True
d. False

218.   What will be the output after the following statements?

```
x = '{} 3 {}'.format('Python', 'Test')
print(x)
```

a. Python 3 Test
b. Python Test
c. Test 3 Python
d. Test Python

219.   What will be the output after the following statements?

```
x = '{1} for {0}'.format('Python', 'Questions')
print(x)
```

a. Python for Questions
b. Questions for Python
c. 1 for 0
d. Python 1 for 0 Questions

220.   What will be the output after the following statements?

```
x = '%s MCQ %s' %('Python', 'Test')
print(x)
```

a. Python MCQ
b. MCQ Test
c. Test MCQ Python
d. Python MCQ Test

221.   What will be the output after the following statements?

```
x = 'Python %d Version' %(3)
print(x)
```

a. Python 3
b. 3 Version
c. Python 3 Version
d. Python Version 3

222.   What will be the output after the following statements?

```
x = 'Python %c or Python %c' %('2', '3')
print(x)
```

a. Python 3 or Python 2
b. Python 2 or Python 3
c. Python 2 or Python 2
d. Python 23

223.   What will be the output after the following statements?

```
x = 'Python %.1f or Python %.2f' %(2.7, 3.51)
print(x)
```

a. Python 3.51 or Python 2.7
b. Python 2 or Python 3
c. Python 2.7 or Python 3.5
d. Python 2.7 or Python 3.51

224.   What will be the output after the following statements?

```
x = 'Python'
print(x.capitalize())
```

a. Python
b. Python.capitalize
c. PYTHON
d. pYTHON

225.   What will be the output after the following statements?

```
x = 'python job interview'
print(x.title())
```

a. python job interview
b. Python job interview
c. Python Job Interview
d. Python job Interview

226.   What will be the output after the following statements?

x = 'python jobs'
print(x.upper())

a. PYTHON JOBS
b. Python jobs
c. Python Jobs
d. python jobs

227.   What will be the output after the following statements?

x = 'python jobs'
print(x.lower())

a. PYTHON JOBS
b. Python jobs
c. Python Jobs
d. python jobs

228.   What will be the output after the following statements?

x = 'Python Jobs'
print(x.swapcase())

a. PYTHON JOBS
b. pYTHON jOBS
c. Python Jobs
d. python jobs

229.   What will be the output after the following statements?

x = 'Python'
print(x.join('33'))

a. Python33
b. 3Python3
c. Python3
d. Python 33

230.   What will be the output after the following statements?

x = 'Python Test'
print(x.join('33'))

a. 3Python Test3
b. 3Python3Test
c. Python3Test3
d. Python Test33

231.   What will be the output after the following statements?

```
x = ' Python '
y = '3'
print(x.lstrip()+y.lstrip())
```

a. Python 3
b. 3Python3
c. Python3
d. Python+3

232.   What will be the output after the following statements?

```
x = 'Python '
y = '3 '
print(x.rstrip()+y.rstrip())
```

a. Python 3
b. 3Python3
c. Python3
d. Python+3

233.   What will be the output after the following statements?

```
x = ' Python '
y = ' 3 '
z = ' Questions '
print(x.strip()+y.strip()+z.strip())
```

a. Python 3 Questions
b. Python3Questions
c. Python3 Questions
d. Python 3Questions

234.   What will be the output after the following statements?

```
x = 'Interview'
print(x.replace('e',' '))
```

a. Interview
b. Intrviw
c. Int e r v i e w
d. Int rvi w

235.   What will be the output after the following statements?

```
x = 'MCQs'
print(x.ljust(10,'*'))
```

a. MCQs******
b. M C Q S
c. ******MCQs
d. M C Q s

236.   What will be the output after the following statements?

```
x = 'MCQs'
print(x.rjust(10,'*'))
```

a. MCQs******
b. M C Q S
c. ******MCQs
d. M C Q s

237.   What will be the output after the following statements?

```
x = 'MCQs'
print(x.center(10,'*'))
```

a. MCQs******
b. ***MCQs***
c. ******MCQs
d. M C Q s

238.   What will be the output after the following statements?

```
x = 'Python Pi Py Pip'
print(x.count('p'))
```

a. 1
b. 0
c. 4
d. 5

239.   What will be the output after the following statements?

```
x = 'Python Pi Py'
print(x.find('p'))
```

a. -1
b. 0
c. 1
d. 3

240.   What will be the output after the following statements?

```
x = 'Python Pi Py'
print(x.find('P'))
```

a. -1
b. 0
c. 1
d. 3

241.   What will be the output after the following statements?

x = 'Pi Py Python'
print(x.startswith('p'))

a. 1
b. 0
c. True
d. False

242.   What will be the output after the following statements?

x = 'Pi Py Python'
print(x.endswith('n'))

a. 1
b. 0
c. True
d. False

243.   What will be the output after the following statements?

x = 'Python'
print(x.isalpha())

a. 1
b. 0
c. True
d. False

244.   What will be the output after the following statements?

x = 'Python 3'
print(x.isnumeric())

a. 1
b. 0
c. True
d. False

245.   What will be the output after the following statements?

x = 'Python 3 MCQ'
print(x.isalnum())

a. 1
b. 0
c. True
d. False

246.   What will be the output after the following statements?

```
x = 'Python 3 MCQ'
print(x.islower())
```

a. True
b. False
c. 1
d. 0

247.   What will be the output after the following statements?

```
x = 'Python 3 MCQ'
print(x.istitle())
```

a. True
b. False
c. 1
d. 0

248.   What will be the output after the following statements?

```
x = 'MCQ'
print(x.isupper())
```

a. True
b. False
c. 1
d. 0

249.   What will be the output after the following statements?

```
x = '\n'
print(x.isspace())
```

a. True
b. False
c. 1
d. 0

250.   What will be the output after the following statements?

```
x = '2000'
print(x.isdigit())
```

a. True
b. False
c. 1
d. 0

251.   What will be the output after the following statements?

x = '2.7'
print(x.isdecimal())

a. True
b. False
c. 1
d. 0

252.   What does the following statement do?

x = open('python.csv', 'r')

a. Opens an existing text file named python.csv to write
b. Opens an existing text file named python.csv to append
c. Opens an existing text file named python.csv to read
d. Opens a new file named python.csv to read

253.   What does the following statement do?

x = open('python.csv', 'w')

a. Opens or creates a text file named python.csv to write
b. Opens or creates a text file named python.csv to append
c. Opens or creates a text file named python.csv to read
d. Opens a new file named python.csv to write

254.   What does the following statement do?

x = open('python.csv', 'a')

a. Opens or creates a text file named python.csv to write
b. Opens or creates a text file named python.csv to append
c. Opens or creates a text file named python.csv to read
d. Opens a new file named python.csv to append

255.   What does the following statement do?

x = open('python.txt', 'r+')

a. Opens a text file named python.txt to read from or write to
b. Opens a text file named python.txt to read
c. Opens a text file named python.txt to write
d. Opens a new file named python.txt to append

256.   What does the following statement do?

x = open('python.txt', 'w+')

a. Opens a text file named python.txt to read
b. Opens a text file named python.txt to write to or read from
c. Opens a text file named python.txt to write
d. Opens a new file named python.txt to append

257.   What does the following statement do?

x = open('python.txt', 'a+')

a. Opens a text file named python.txt to read
b. Opens a text file named python.txt to read and write
c. Opens a text file named python.txt to write to
d. Opens or creates a text file named python.txt to read from or write to at the end of the file

258.   What does the following statement do?

x = open('python.bat', 'rb')

a. Opens an existing text file named python.bat to write
b. Opens an existing binary file named python.bat to write
c. Opens an existing binary file named python.bat to append
d. Opens an existing binary file named python.bat to read

259.   What does the following statement do?

x = open('python.bat', 'wb')

a. Opens or creates a binary file named python.bat to write
b. Opens or creates a binary file named python.bat to append
c. Opens or creates a binary file named python.bat to read
d. Opens a new file named python.bat to write

260.   What does the following statement do?

x = open('python.bat', 'ab')

a. Opens or creates a binary file named python.bat to write
b. Opens or creates a binary file named python.bat to append
c. Opens or creates a binary file named python.bat to read
d. Opens a new file named python.bat to append

261.   What will be the output after the following statements?

x = open('python.txt', 'r')
print(x.name)

a. python
b. python.txt opened
c. python.txt or FileNotFoundError
d. python r

262.   What will be the output after the following statements?

x = open('python.csv', 'w')
print(x.mode)

a. python write
b. python.txt
c. r
d. w

263.   What will be the output after the following statements?

x = open('python.csv', 'w')
print(x.closed)

a. open
b. closed
c. True
d. False

264.   What will be the output after the following statements?

x = open('python.csv', 'w')
x.close()
print(x.closed)

a. open
b. closed
c. True
d. False

265.   What will be the output after the following statements?

x = open('python.csv', 'w')
print(x.readable())

a. readable
b. writable
c. True
d. False

266.   What will be the output after the following statements?

x = open('python.csv', 'w')

print(x.writable())

a. readable
b. writable
c. True
d. False

267.   What will be the output after the following statements?

```
x = open('python.csv', 'a')
print(x.writable())
```

a. readable
b. writable
c. True
d. False

268.   In IDLE shell, the output will be the same for all the following statements except one. Which one?

a. 4+4
b. 4 + 4
c. 4*2
d. 4**2

269.   In IDLE shell, what is the keyboard shortcut for the previous command in history on Windows/Linux?

a. Page Down
b. Page Up
c. Alt + P
d. Ctrl + P

270.   In IDLE shell, what is the keyboard shortcut for the next command in history on Windows/Linux?

a. Page Down
b. Page Up
c. Ctrl + N
d. Alt + N

271.   In IDLE shell, what is the keyboard shortcut for the previous command in history on Mac OS X?

a. Page Down
b. Page Up
c. Alt + P
d. Ctrl + P

272.   In IDLE shell, what is the keyboard shortcut for the next command in history on Mac OS

X?

- a. Page Down
- b. Page Up
- c. Ctrl + N
- d. Alt + N

273.   In IDLE file editor, what is the keyboard shortcut for executing the program in shell?

- a. F5
- b. F1
- c. Shift
- d. Alt

274.   What type of error is shown when you use a variable without assigning an initial value?

- a. Not declared
- b. Not defined
- c. Not assigned
- d. Not a variable

275.   What type of language is Python?

- a. High level
- b. Low level
- c. Top level
- d. Bottom level

276.   Python language was named after?

- a. Python - the reptile
- b. Monty Python
- c. A pet
- d. A company

277.   Who is the creator of Python?

- a. Bill Gates
- b. Guido Van Rossum
- c. Jeff Bezos
- d. Larry Page

278.   Which of the following is identified with Python?

- a. Dynamic typing
- b. Static typing
- c. Slow typing
- d. Auto typing

279.   Which of the following is used to enclose strings?

a. Single quotes
b. Double quotes
c. Either single quotes or double quotes
d. ! symbol

280.   Which of the following is used to add an invisible tab character to the output?

a. \t
b. \tab
c. \a
d. \b

281.   What will be the output after the following statement?

print('2\\t4')

a. 2 t 4
b. 2\t4
c. 2 4
d. 2 tab 4

282.   What will be the output after the following statements?

a = True
b = False
c = 5 if (a == 1) else b
print(c)

a. True
b. False
c. b
d. 5

283.   What will be the output after the following statements?

a = True
b = False
c = 'a' if (b == 0) else 'b'
print(c)

a. True
b. False
c. a
d. b

284.   What will be the output after the following statements?

a = False
b = False

print(a and b)

a. True
b. False
c. ab
d. ba

285. In the order of precedence, which of the operation will be completed first in the following statement?

3 * 6 + 5 - 4 / 2

a. Multiplication
b. Division
c. Addition
d. Subtraction

286. In the order of precedence, which of the operation will be completed last in the following statement?

3 * 6 + 5 - 4 / 2

a. Multiplication
b. Division
c. Addition
d. Subtraction

287. What will be the order of precedence of operations in the following statement?

10 * 4 - 1 + 8 / 5

a. Multiplication, Division, Subtraction, Addition
b. Multiplication, Division, Addition, Subtraction
c. Division, Multiplication, Subtraction, Addition
d. Division, Multiplication, Addition, Subtraction

288. What will be the data type of x after the following statement if input entered is 64?

x = float(input('Enter a number: '))

a. Integer
b. String
c. List
d. Float

289. What will be the output after the following statements?

a = 27 / 3 % 2 * 4**2
print(a)

a. 0
b. 16.0
c. 32
d. 4.0

290.   What will be the output after the following statements?

a = 3 / 3 * 47 - 3**3
print(a)

a. 20.0
b. 1.0
c. 36.0
d. 0.0

291.   What will be the output after the following statements?

a = [1,3,5,7,9,11,13,15,17,19]
print(a[1:5],a[3:17])

a. [3, 5, 7, 9]
b. [1, 3, 5] [3, 5, 7, 9, 11, 13, 15, 17]
c. [3, 5, 7, 9] [7, 9, 11, 13, 15, 17, 19]
d. [3, 5, 7, 9, 11, 13, 15, 17, 19]

292.   What will be the output after the following statements?

a = [1,3,5]
print(a * 2)

a. [1, 3, 5, 1, 3, 5]
b. [1, 2, 3, 5]
c. [3, 5]
d. [11, 33, 55]

293.   Which of the following is not a valid variable name?

a. abc
b. abc123
c. 123abc
d. abc_123

294.   Which of the following is a valid variable name?

a. a$1
b. a1
c. 1a
d. abc 123

295.   What will be the output after the following statements?

```
a = 15
b = a
a = 25
print(a,b)
```

a. 25 15
b. 15 25
c. a 15
d. 25 a

296.   What will be the output after the following statements?

```
x = 16 / 4 * 5
y = 16 / 4 * 5.0
z = 16 / 4.0 * 5
print(x, y, z)
```

a. 25 15 20
b. 20.0 20.0 20.0
c. 20.0 20 20.0
d. 20 20.0 20

297.   What will be the data type of x after the following statement?

```
x = 1/2
```

a. Integer
b. List
c. String
d. Float

298.   What will be the output after the following statements?

```
def x(y,z):
    pass
x(1,4)
```

a. 1,4
b. y,z
c. No output
d. None

299.   What will be the output after the following statements?

```
b = 1
for a in range(1, 10, 3):
    b += a + 1
print(b)
```

a. 14
b. 16
c. 20
d. 25

300.   What will be the output after the following statements?

```
b = 1
for a in range(1, 10):
    b += a - 1
print(b)
```

a. 37
b. 47
c. 44
d. 38

301.   What will be the output after the following statements?

```
b = 3
for a in range(10, 1):
    b -= a + 1
print(b)
```

a. 7
b. 4
c. 3
d. 8

302.   What will be the output after the following statements?

```
b = 1
for a in range(1, 5):
    b *= a + 1
print(b)
```

a. 120
b. 40
c. 36
d. 250

303.   What will be the output after the following statements?

```
a = True
print(a and not a)
```

a. a
b. False
c. not a
d. True

304.   What will be the output after the following statements?

```
a = True
b = False
print(a == b or not b)
```

a. a == b
b. False
c. not b
d. True

305.   What will be the output after the following statements?

```
a = 'Hello'
b = 'hello'
print(a is b)
```

a. a is b
b. False
c. not b
d. True

306.   What will be the output after the following statements?

```
a = 'Python'
b = 'Python'
print(a is b)
```

a. a is b
b. False
c. not b
d. True

307.   What will be the output after the following statements?

```
a = [4, 7, 9]
b = [4, 7, 9]
print(a is b)
```

a. a is b
b. False
c. not b
d. True

308.   What will be the output after the following statements?

```
a = [4, 7, 9]
b = [7, 4, 9]
print(a is not b)
```

a. a is b
b. False
c. not b
d. True

309. What will be the output after the following statements?

```
a = [3, 6, 9]
b = [3, 6, 9]
print(a is b, a == b)
```

a. True True
b. False False
c. False True
d. True False

310. What will be the output after the following statements?

```
a = 0
b = 5
c = 10
a = b
b = c
c = a
print(a, b, c)
```

a. 0 5 10
b. 5 10 10
c. 5 10 5
d. 5 5 10

311. What will be the output after the following statements?

```
b = 15
c = 20
a = b
b = c
c = a
print(b, c)
```

a. 20 15
b. 15 20
c. a 20
d. 15 a

312. In IDLE shell, the output will be the same for all the following statements except one. Which one?

a. 4*3

b. 60//5
c. 17-5
d. 12/1

313.   In IDLE shell, the output will be an error for one of the following statements. Which one?

a. P = 'python' * int('1')
b. P = 'python' + 1
c. P = 'python' + str(1)
d. P = 'python' * 1

314.   What will be the output after the following statements?

```
a = 4**3
b = pow(4,3)
print(a, b)
```

a. 4 4
b. 4 3
c. 12 12
d. 64 64

315.   What will be the output after the following statements?

```
a = min(10, 15, 6, 17, 24)
print(a)
```

a. (10, 15, 6, 17, 24)
b. 6
c. 5
d. 24

316.   What will be the output after the following statements?

```
a = [4, 25, 16, 9, 24]
print(max(a))
```

a. [4, 25, 16, 9, 24]
b. 9
c. 25
d. 24

317.   What will be the output after the following statements?

```
a = round(5.3)
b = round(5.6)
c = round(5.5)
print(a, b, c)
```

a. 5 5 5

b. 6 5 6
c. 5 6 6
d. 5 6 5

318.   How many times will "Python 3" be printed after the following statements?

```
for i in range(1, 5):
    print('Python 3')
```

a. 3
b. 4
c. 5
d. 6

319.   What will be the output after the following statements?

```
a = round(4.49999)
print(a)
```

a. 4
b. 5
c. 4.0
d. 4.5

320.   What will be the output for a function that does not return any value?

a. None
b. No value
c. Zero
d. Bool

321.   What type of error will be shown after the following statement?

```
a = b
```

a. SyntaxError
b. TypeError
c. ValueError
d. NameError

322.   What type of error will be shown after the following statement?

```
a = int('hello')
```

a. SyntaxError
b. TypeError
c. ValueError
d. NameError

323.   What type of error will be shown after the following statement?

a = {7)

a. SyntaxError
b. TypeError
c. ValueError
d. NameError

324. What type of error will be shown after the following statement?

a = 'Python' + 3

a. SyntaxError
b. TypeError
c. ValueError
d. NameError

325. What is the data type of a after the following statement?

a = {'A', 'B', 'C', 'D'}

a. List
b. Dictionary
c. Tuple
d. Set

326. What is the data type of a after the following statement?

a = {'A':1, 'B':2, 'C':3, 'D':4}

a. List
b. Dictionary
c. Tuple
d. Set

327. What is the data type of a after the following statement?

a = (1, 4, 3, 6)

a. List
b. Dictionary
c. Tuple
d. Set

328. What is the data type of a after the following statement?

a = [1, 4, 3, 6]

a. List
b. Dictionary

c. Tuple

d. Set

329.   What is the data type used to store values in key values pair?

a. List

b. Dictionary

c. Tuple

d. Set

330.   In IDLE shell, which of the following statements gives SyntaxError?

a. "Python\tis\tEasy\n"

b. "Hello, it's very easy to learn Python"

c. "Python", "easy"

d. "Python is easy'

331.   What will be the output after the following statements?

```
a = 45
b = 55
c = (a + b) / 2
print(c)
```

a. 45

b. 50.0

c. 45.0

d. 55.0

332.   Which of the following has the highest precedence in an expression?

a. Parentheses

b. Exponential

c. Division

d. Subtraction

333.   What will be the output after the following statements?

```
a = 4*3**2
print(a)
```

a. 32

ba. 144

c. 36

d. 24

334.   What is the name of Python's built-in module for regular expressions?

a. regex

b. regexes

c. REG

d. re

335.   What is the name of Python's built-in module for delimited files?

a. csv

b. tsc

c. delimited

d. pipe

336.   What is the name of Python's built-in module for basic date and time types?

a. date

b. time

c. datetime

d. dates

337.   What is the name of Python's built-in module for email related tasks?

a. mailserver

b. email

c. message

d. mail

338.   What is the name of Python's built-in module for reading passwords?

a. getpass

b. password

c. login

d. readpass

339.   What is the name of Python's built-in module for IPv4/IPv6 manipulation?

a. getip

b. ipman

c. ip

d. ipaddress

340.   What is the name of Python's built-in module for encoding/decoding JSON format?

a. json

b. jcode

c. jsonencode

d. jsoncode

341.   What is the name of Python's built-in module for Python keywords?

a. string

b. keyword

c. stringtest

d. keytest

342. What is the name of Python's built-in module for mathematical functions?

a. maths
b. mathematics
c. math
d. mathfunc

343. What is the name of Python's built-in module for operating system interfaces?

a. windows
b. liunx
c. operatingsystem
d. os

344. What is the name of Python's built-in module for data pretty printer?

a. pprint
b. print
c. prettyprint
d. printp

345. What is the name of Python's built-in module for generating pseudo-random numbers?

a. psrandom
b. random
c. psuedo
d. randomnum

346. What is the name of Python's built-in module for general purpose event scheduler?

a. scheduler
b. eventsched
c. sched
d. schedule

347. What is the name of Python's built-in module for high level file operations?

a. shutil
b. fileutil
c. futility
d. fileop

348. What is the name of Python's built-in module for low level networking interface?

a. net
b. socket
c. webking
d. webworking

349. What is the name of Python's built-in module for SQLite databases?

a. SQL
b. sqldb
c. dbase
d. sqlite3

350. What is the name of Python's built-in module for TLS/SSL wrapper for socket objects?

a. ssl
b. swrap
c. tlsssl
d. sslobj

351. What is the name of Python's built-in module for mathematical statistics functions?

a. mathstats
b. statistics
c. statmath
d. statfunc

352. What is the name of Python's built-in module for subprocess management?

a. sub
b. mansub
c. submng
d. subprocess

353. What is the name of Python's built-in module for Python's configuration information?

a. config
b. pysys
c. sysconfig
d. pycon

354. What is the name of Python's built-in module for telnet client class?

a. telnetlib
b. tellib
c. tnet
d. telnet

355. What is the name of Python's built-in module for generating temporary files and directories?

a. temp
b. tempdir
c. temporary
d. tempfile

356.   What is the name of Python's built-in module for thread based parallelism?

a. thread
b. threadall
c. threading
d. thrpar

357.   What is the name of Python's built-in module for time access and conversions?

a. timely
b. time
c. primetime
d. mytime

358.   What is the name of Python's built-in module for working with calendars?

a. calendars
b. calendar
c. yearcal
d. calc

359.   What is the name of Python's built-in module for measuring execution time of code snippets?

a. timeit
b. selftime
c. codetime
d. timer

360.   What is the name of Python's built-in module for interface to Tcl/Tk for graphical user interfaces?

a. tkgui
b. guitk
c. intertk
d. tkinter

361.   What is the name of Python's built-in module for simple educational graphical applications?

a. torque
b. tedu
c. turtle
d. moveturtle

362.   What is the name of Python's built-in module for url handling?

a. urls
b. urllib
c. URL

d. httpurl

363. What is the name of Python's built-in module for interface to WAV sound format?

a. wav
b. WAVE
c. WAV
d. wave

364. What is the name of Python's built-in module for web browser controlller?

a. browser
b. browse
c. webrowser
d. webbrowser

365. What is the name of Python's built-in module for xml processing?

a. xml
b. XML
c. allxml
d. onlyxml

366. What is the name of Python's built-in module for reading and writing ZIP archive files?

a. readzip
b. zipfile
c. writezip
d. rwzip

367. What is the name of Python's built-in module for running Python scripts via CGI?

a. pcgi
b. pycgi
c. cgi
d. cgipy

368. What is the name of Python's built-in module for mathematical functions for complex numbers?

a. complexmath
b. cmath
c. mathc
d. mathplex

369. What is the name of Python's built-in module for conversions between color systems?

a. color
b. colors
c. colours

d. colorsys

370. What is the name of Python's built-in module for shallow and deep copy operations?

a. copyd
b. copyme
c. copy
d. copys

371. What is the name of Python's built-in module for comparing files?

a. filecmp
b. cmpfile
c. compare
d. filecompare

372. What is the name of Python's built-in module for FTP protocol client?

a. ftp
b. ftplib
c. FTP
d. pftp

373. What is the name of Python's built-in module for unix style pathname pattern expansion?

a. upattern
b. pathpat
c. upath
d. glob

374. What is the name of Python's built-in module for html manipulation?

a. hyper
b. xml
c. html
d. uml

375. What will be the output after the following statements?

```
x = [5, 4, 3, 2, 1]
x.clear()
print(x)
```

a. [0, 1, 2, 3, 4, 5]
b. [0]
c. []
d. [1, 2, 3, 4, 5]

376. What will be the output after the following statements?

```
x = [5, 4, 3, 2, 1]
y = x.copy()
print(y)
```

a. [0, 1, 2, 3, 4, 5]
b. [5, 4, 3, 2, 1]
c. []
d. [1, 2, 3, 4, 5]

377.   What will be the output after the following statements?

```
x = []
for i in range(10):
    x.append(i**2)
print(x)
```

a. [0, 1, 2, 3, 4, 5]
b. [0, 1, 4, 9, 16, 25, 36, 49, 64, 81]
c. [0, 1, 4, 9, 16, 25, 36, 49, 64, 81, 100]
d. [1, 4, 9, 16, 25, 36, 49, 64, 81]

378.   What will be the output after the following statements?

```
x = list(map(lambda x:x**2, range(5)))
print(x)
```

a. [0, 1, 2, 3, 4, 5]
b. [1, 4, 9, 16, 25]
c. [0, 1, 4, 9, 16, 25]
d. [0, 1, 4, 9, 16]

379.   What will be the output after the following statements?

```
x = [i**2 for i in range(4)]
print(x)
```

a. [0, 1, 2, 3, 4, 5]
b. [1, 4, 9]
c. [0, 1, 4, 9]
d. [0, 1, 4, 9, 16]

380.   What will be the output after the following statements?

```
a = [(x, y) for x in [0, 1, 2] for y in [3, 4, 5] if x!=y]
print(a)
```

a. [0, 1, 2, 3, 4, 5]
b. [(1, 3), (1, 4), (1, 5), (2, 3), (2, 4), (2, 5)]
c. [(0, 1, 2), (3, 4, 5)]
d. [(0, 3), (0, 4), (0, 5), (1, 3), (1, 4), (1, 5), (2, 3), (2, 4), (2, 5)]

381. What will be the output after the following statements?

```
a = [(x, y) for x in [0, 3, 5] for y in [5, 4, 0] if x!=y]
print(a)
```

a. [(0, 5), (0, 4), (3, 5), (3, 4), (3, 0), (5, 4), (5, 0)]
b. [(1, 3), (1, 4), (1, 5), (2, 3), (2, 4), (2, 5)]
c. [(0, 3, 5), (0, 4, 5)]
d. [(0, 5), (0, 4), (0, 0), (3, 5), (3, 4), (3, 0), (5, 5), (5, 4), (5, 0)]

382. What will be the output after the following statements?

```
a = [(x, y) for x in [0, 2] for y in [2, 4, 0] if x==y]
print(a)
```

a. [(0, 2)]
b. [(0, 0), (2, 2)]
c. [(0, 2), (2, 4, 0)]
d. [(0, 2), (0, 4), (0, 0), (2, 2), (2, 4), (2, 0)]

383. What will be the output after the following statements?

```
a = [(x, y) for x in [0, 2] for y in [2, 4, 0] if x!=y]
print(a)
```

a. [(0, 2)]
b. [(0, 0), (2, 2)]
c. [(0, 2), (0, 4), (2, 4), (2, 0)]
d. [(0, 2), (0, 4), (0, 0), (2, 2), (2, 4), (2, 0)]

384. What will be the output after the following statements?

```
a = []
for x in [0, 1, 2]:
    for y in [3, 4, 5]:
        if x!=y:
            a.append((x,y))
print(a)
```

a. [0, 1, 2, 3, 4, 5]
b. [(1, 3), (1, 4), (1, 5), (2, 3), (2, 4), (2, 5)]
c. [(0, 1, 2), (3, 4, 5)]
d. [(0, 3), (0, 4), (0, 5), (1, 3), (1, 4), (1, 5), (2, 3), (2, 4), (2, 5)]

385. What will be the output after the following statements?

```
a = [-2, -1, 0, 1, 2]
print([i**3 for i in a])
```

a. [(0, 2)]
b. [-2, -1, 0, 1, 2]
c. [8, 1, 0, 1, 8]
d. [-8, -1, 0, 1, 8]

386.   What will be the output after the following statements?

a = [-3, -1, 0, 1, 3]
print([i**4 for i in a])

a. [81, 1, 0, 1, 81]
b. [-81, -1, 0, 1, 81]
c. [16, 1, 0, 1, 16]
d. [-16, -1, 0, 1, 16]

387.   What will be the output after the following statements?

a = [-3, -1, 0, 1, 3]
print([x for x in a if x>=0])

a. [-3, -1, 0, 1, 3]
b. [0, 1, 3]
c. [1, 3]
d. [-1, 0, 1]

388.   What will be the output after the following statements?

a = [-3, -1, 0, 1, 3]
print([abs(x) for x in a])

a. [-3, -1, 0, 1, 3]
b. [0, 1, 3]
c. [3, 1, 0, 1, 3]
d. [-1, 0, 1]

389.   What will be the output after the following statements?

a = [' today', ' tomorrow ', 'not now']
print([x.strip() for x in a])

a. ['today', 'tomorrow ', 'not now']
b. [' today', ' tomorrow', 'not now']
c. ['today', 'tomorrow', 'notnow']
d. ['today', 'tomorrow', 'not now']

390.   What will be the output after the following statements?

print([(x, x*2) for x in range(4)])

a. [(0, 0), (1, 2), (2, 4), (3, 6)]

b. [(0, 0), (1, 2), (2, 4), (3, 6), (4, 8)]
c. [(1, 2), (2, 4), (3, 6), (4, 8)]
d. [(1, 2), (2, 4), (3, 6)]

391.   What will be the output after the following statements?

a = [[0, 1, 2], [7, 8, 9], [4, 5, 6]]
print([x for y in a for x in y])

a. [0, 1, 2, 4, 5, 6, 7, 8, 9]
b. [0, 1, 2, 7, 8, 9, 4, 5, 6]
c. [(0, 1, 2), (7, 8, 9), (4, 5, 6)]
d. [(0, 7, 4), (1, 8, 5), (2, 9, 6)]

392.   What will be the output after the following statements?

from math import pi
a = [str(round(pi, i)) for i in range(0,5)]
print(a)

a. [3.0, 3.1, 3.14, 3.142, 3.1416]
b. ['3.0', '3.1', '3.14', '3.142']
c. ['3.0', '3.1', '3.14', '3.142', '3.1416']
d. ['3.1', '3.14', '3.142', '3.1416']

393.   What will be the output after the following statements?

a = [[0, 1, 2, 3], [4, 5, 6, 7], [8, 9, 10, 11]]
b = [[x[i] for x in a] for i in range(4)]
print(b)

a. [0, 1, 2, 3, 4, 5, 6, 7, 8, 9, 10, 11]
b. [[0, 4, 8], [1, 5, 9], [2, 6, 10], [3, 7, 11]]
c. [[0, 1, 2], [3, 4, 5], [6, 7, 8], [9, 10, 11]]
d. [0, 1, 2, 3], [4, 5, 6, 7], [8, 9, 10, 11]

394.   What will be the output after the following statements?

a = []
b = [[0, 1, 2, 3], [4, 5, 6, 7], [8, 9, 10, 11]]
for i in range(4):
    a.append([row[i] for row in b])
print(a)

a. [0, 1, 2, 3, 4, 5, 6, 7, 8, 9, 10, 11]
b. [[0, 4, 8], [1, 5, 9], [2, 6, 10], [3, 7, 11]]
c. [[0, 1, 2], [3, 4, 5], [6, 7, 8], [9, 10, 11]]
d. [0, 1, 2, 3], [4, 5, 6, 7], [8, 9, 10, 11]

395.   What will be the output after the following statements?

```
a = [[0, 1, 2, 3], [4, 5, 6, 7], [8, 9, 10, 11]]
print(list(zip(*a)))
```

a. [0, 1, 2, 3, 4, 5, 6, 7, 8, 9, 10, 11]
b. [[0, 4, 8], [1, 5, 9], [2, 6, 10], [3, 7, 11]]
c. [[0, 1, 2], [3, 4, 5], [6, 7, 8], [9, 10, 11]]
d. [0, 1, 2, 3], [4, 5, 6, 7], [8, 9, 10, 11]

396.   What will be the output after the following statements?

```
a = [0, 1, 2, 3]
del a
print(a)
```

a. None
b. Null
c. [0, 1, 2, 3]
d. NameError

397.   What will be the output after the following statements?

```
a = [0, 1, 2, 3]
del a[:]
print(a)
```

a. None
b. []
c. [0, 1, 2, 3]
d. NameError

398.   What will be the output after the following statements?

```
x = [i*2-4 for i in range(5)]
print(x)
```

a. [0, 1, 2, 3, 4, 5]
b. [0, 1, 2, 3, 4]
c. [-4, -2, 0, 2, 4]
d. [0, 1, 4, 9, 16]

399.   What will be the output after the following statements?

```
x = [i**2-3 for i in range(0,7,3)]
print(x)
```

a. [-3, 6, 33]
b. [0, 1, 2, 3, 4]
c. [-3, -2, 0, 2, 3]
d. [-3, 9, 18, 36]

400. What will be the output after the following statements?

```
x = [i**4//7 for i in range(0,6,2)]
print(x)
```

   a. [0, 2, 36]
   b. [0, 1, 2, 3, 4]
   c. [0, 6, 2]
   d. [0, 2, 14]

401. What will be the output after the following statements?

```
x = [int(i**3/3) for i in range(0,5,2)]
print(x)
```

   a. [0, 2, 36]
   b. [0, 2, 21]
   c. [0, 6, 2]
   d. [0, 2, 14]

402. What will be the output after the following statements?

```
x = [int(i/2-5) for i in range(3,8,2)]
print(x)
```

   a. [-3, -2, -1]
   b. [0, 2, 6]
   c. [0, 1, 2]
   d. [-3, -1, 3]

403. What is the famous one-line Hello World program of Python?

   a. print("Hello World!")
   b. print "Hello World!"
   c. print("Hello World!")!
   d. print("Hello World!"):

404. What is used for multi-line strings in Python?

   a. Three braces {{{ }}}
   b. Three Colons ::: :::
   c. Three hashes ### ###
   d. Three Quotes ''' '''

405. What will be the output after the following statements?

```
x = 90
y = 'I ran for %s minutes'
print(y % x)
```

a. y ran for x minutes
b. y ran for 90 minutes
c. I ran for 90 minutes
d. I ran for x minutes

406.   What will be the output after the following statements?

```
x = 'She'
y = 60
z = 'ran for %s minutes'
print(x, z % y)
```

a. ran for 60 minutes
b. she ran for 60 minutes
c. She ran for 60 minutes
d. x ran for 60 minutes

407.   What will be the output after the following statements?

```
x = 75
y = 60
z = 'ran for %s minutes'
print(z % y)
```

a. ran for 75 minutes
b. ran for 60 minutes
c. ran for 135 minutes
d. y ran for 60 minutes

408.   What will be the output after the following statements?

```
x = 7
y = 6
z = 'He ran for %s minutes for %s days'
print(z % (x, y))
```

a. He ran for 7 minutes for 7 days
b. He ran for 6 minutes for 6 days
c. He ran for 6 minutes for 7 days
d. He ran for 7 minutes for 6 days

409.   What will be the output after the following statements?

```
x = 'Python 2'
y = 'Python 3'
z = 'We can convert %s program to %s program'
print(z % (x, y))
```

a. We can not convert Python 2 program to Python 3 program

b. We can not convert Python 3 program to Python 2 program
c. We can convert Python 2 program to Python 3 program
d. We can convert Python 3 program to Python 2 program

410.   What will be the output after the following statements?

```
x = ''
print(x*5)
```

a. Displays a tab
b. Displays 5 spaces
c. Displays a newline
d. Displays 10 quotes

411.   What will be the output after the following statements?

```
x = 'no'
y = 'yes'
z = 'may be'
a = [y, z, x]
print(a)
```

a. 'yes', 'may be', 'no'
b. 'no', 'may be', 'yes'
c. ['no', 'may be', 'yes']
d. ['yes', 'may be', 'no']

412.   Which of the following operations is not possible while manipulating lists?

a. Addition
b. Multiplication
c. Division
d. Deletion

413.   Which of the following is used by interpreter to identify code blocks?

a. Braces
b. Indentation
c. Commas
d. Expressions

414.   What will be the output after the following statements?

```
x = ["Yesterday's", "Today's", "Tomorrow's"]
y = ['weather', 'temperature', 'humidity']
for i in x:
   print(i, end=' ')
for j in y:
     print(j, end=' ')
```

a. Yesterday's Today's Tomorrow's weather temperature humidity
b. Yesterday's weather temperature humidity
c. Yesterday's weather temperature humidity Today's Tomorrow's
d. Yesterday's weather Today's temperature Tomorrow's humidity

415.   What will be the output after the following statements?

```
x = ["Yesterday's", "Today's", "Tomorrow's"]
y = ['temperature']
for i in x:
    print(i, end=' ')
    for j in y:
        print(j, end=' ')
```

a. Yesterday's Today's Tomorrow's temperature
b. Yesterday's temperature
c. Yesterday's temperature Today's Tomorrow's
d. Yesterday's temperature Today's temperature Tomorrow's temperature

416.   What will be the output after the following statements?

```
x = ["Yesterday's", "Today's", "Tomorrow's"]
y = ['temperature']
for i in x:
    if i[0] == 'T':
        for j in y:
            print(i, j, end=' ')
```

a. Today's Tomorrow's temperature
b. Today's temperature Tomorrow's temperature
c. temperature Today's Tomorrow's
d. Today's temperature Tomorrow's

417.   What will be the output after the following statements?

```
x = ["Yesterday's", "Today's", "Tomorrow's"]
y = ['temperature']
for i in x:
    if i[0] != 'T':
        for j in y:
            print(i, end=' ')
```

a. Today's Tomorrow's temperature
b. Yesterday's temperature Tomorrow's temperature
c. Yesterday's
d. Yesterday's Today's Tomorrow's

418.   What will be the output after the following statements?

```
x = ["Yesterday's", "Today's", "Tomorrow's"]
```

```
y = ['temperature']
for i in x:
    if i[0] != 'y':
        for j in y:
            print(j, end=' ')
```

a. temperature temperature
b. temperature
c. temperature temperature temperature
d. Yesterday's Today's Tomorrow's

419.   What will be the output after the following statements?

```
x = 25
y = 10
while x < 26 and y < 11:
    x = x + 1
    y = y + 1
    print(x,y)
```

a. 26 11
b. 25 11
c. 25 10
d. 26 10

420.   What will be the output after the following statements?

```
x = 25
y = 10
while x < 26 and y < 11:
    print(x,y)
    x = x + 1
    y = y + 1
```

a. 26 11
b. 25 11
c. 25 10
d. 26 10

421.   What will be the output after the following statement?

print(list(range(0,5)))

a. list(range(0,5))
b. list(0, 1, 2, 3, 4)
c. 0, 1, 2, 3, 4
d. [0, 1, 2, 3, 4]

422.   What will be the output after the following statements?

```
def abc(world):
    print('hello %s' % world)
abc('Python')
```

a. hello world
b. hello Python
c. hello
d. hello % world

423.   What will be the output after the following statements?

```
def abc(x, y):
    print('hello %s %s' % (y, x))
abc('Python', 'world')
```

a. hello world
b. hello Python world
c. hello Python
d. hello world Python

424.   What will be the output after the following statements?

```
b = 'Python'
a = 'world'
def pypi(x, y):
    print('hello %s %s' % (y, x))
pypi(a, b)
```

a. hello world
b. hello Python world
c. hello Python
d. hello world Python

425.   What will be the output after the following statements?

```
a = 12
b = 45
c = 10
def pypi(x, y, z):
    return(z * y - x)
print(pypi(b, c, a))
```

a. 15
b. 45
c. 75
d. 120

426.   What will be the output after the following statements?

```
def pypi():
```

```
   b = 25
   c = 20
   return(a * b - c)
a = 12
print(pypi())
```

a. 280
b. Error
c. 60
d. 215

427.   What will be the output after the following statements?

```
class Furniture:
   def legs(x):
      print('has %s legs' % x)
Furniture.legs(4)
```

a. Furniture has 4 legs
b. Error
c. has 4 legs
d. legs has 4 legs

428.   What will be the output after the following statements?

```
class Furniture:
   def legs():
      print('is made of wood')
Furniture.legs()
```

a. Furniture is made of wood
b. is made of wood
c. print(is made of wood)
d. legs is made of wood

429.   What will be the output after the following statements?

```
class Furniture:
   def chair(x):
      print('It has %s legs' % x)
   def table(x):
      print('It has %s legs' % x)
Furniture.table(6)
```

a. It has 4 legs
b. It has no legs
c. It has 0 legs
d. It has 6 legs

430.   What will be the output after the following statements?

```
class Furniture:
    def chair():
        print('It has 4 legs')
    def table():
        print('It has 6 legs')
Furniture.chair()
```

a. It has 4 legs
b. It has no legs
c. It has 0 legs
d. It has 6 legs

431.   What will be the output after the following statements?

```
x = -4
if abs(x) > 0:
    print('This is absolute value')
```

a. None
b. Error
c. Wrong Value
d. This is absolute value

432.   What will be the output after the following statements?

```
x = -3
if abs(x) < 3:
    print(x)
else:
    print(0)
```

a. No output
b. Error
c. 0
d. -3

433.   What will be the output after the following statements?

```
x = -4
if bool(x):
    print(x)
else:
    print(0)
```

a. No output
b. Error
c. 0
d. -4

434. What will be the output after the following statements?

```
x = 0
if bool(x):
    print(x)
else:
    print(5)
```

a. No output
b. Error
c. 5
d. 0

435. What will be the output after the following statements?

```
x = 'None'
if bool(x):
    print('Yes')
else:
    print('No')
```

a. None
b. Yes
c. No
d. 0

436. What will be the output after the following statements?

```
x = "
if bool(x):
    print('Yes')
else:
    print('No')
```

a. None
b. Yes
c. No
d. 0

437. What will be the output after the following statements?

```
x = ''
if bool(x):
    print('Yes')
else:
    print('No')
```

a. None
b. Yes
c. No

d. 0

438. What will be the output after the following statements?

```
x = []
if bool(x):
    print('Yes')
else:
    print('No')
```

a. No
b. Yes
c. None
d. 0

439. What will be the output after the following statements?

```
x = [1, 2, 3]
if bool(x):
    print('Yes')
else:
    print('No')
```

a. No
b. Yes
c. None
d. 0

440. What will be the output after the following statements?

```
x = "
if not bool(x):
    print('Yes')
else:
    print('No')
```

a. Yes
b. No
c. None
d. 0

441. What will be the output after the following statements?

```
x = 'print("Python")'
eval(x)
```

a. x
b. print("Python")
c. Python
d. 0

442.   What will be the output after the following statements if input entered is 45*2?

```
x = input("Enter an expression: ")
print(eval(x))
```

a. 45*2
b. eval("90")
c. 90
d. 0

443.   What will be the output after the following statements?

```
x = '''print("Python 3", end='')
print(" is Good")'''
exec(x)
```

a. Python 3is Good
b. Python 3 is Good
c. Python 3
d. is Good

444.   What will be the output after the following statements?

```
a = ['a', 'b', 'c', 'A', 'B']
print(max(a))
```

a. a
b. A
c. b
d. c

445.   What will be the output after the following statements?

```
a = ['a', 'b', 'c', 'A', 'B']
print(min(a))
```

a. a
b. A
c. b
d. c

446.   What will be the output after the following statements?

```
a = ['a', 'b', 'c', '1', '2', 'A', 'B']
print(max(a))
```

a. a
b. A
c. 1

d. c

447.   What will be the output after the following statements?

```
a = ['a', 'b', 'c', '1', '2', 'A', 'B']
print(min(a))
```

a. a
b. A
c. 1
d. c

448.   What will be the output after the following statements?

```
a = [1, 2, 3]
print(sum(a))
```

a. 3
b. 2
c. 1
d. 6

449.   What will be the output after the following statements?

```
a = list(range(0,10,3))
print(sum(a))
```

a. 10
b. 100
c. 18
d. 30

450.   What will be the output after the following statements?

```
a = list(range(10,-10,3))
print(sum(a))
```

a. 10
b. 0
c. 18
d. 90

451.   What will be the output after the following statements?

```
a = list(range(-10,5,2))
print(sum(a))
```

a. -24
b. 0
c. 24

d. 20

452.   What will be the output after the following statements?

```
x = [5, 4, 3, 2, 1]
y = x.copy()
x[0] = 6
print(y)
```

a. [6, 4, 3, 2, 1]
b. 6
c. [5, 4, 3, 2, 1]
d. 5

453.   What will be the output after the following statements?

```
import copy
x = [5, 4, 3, 2, 1]
y = copy.copy(x)
x.append(6)
print(y[0])
```

a. [6, 4, 3, 2, 1]
b. 6
c. [5, 4, 3, 2, 1]
d. 5

454.   What will be the output after the following statements?

```
import keyword
print(keyword.iskeyword('IS'))
```

a. True
b. keyword
c. for
d. False

455.   What will be the output after the following statements?

```
import keyword
print(keyword.iskeyword('for'))
```

a. True
b. keyword
c. for
d. False

456.   What will be the output after the following statements?

```
import keyword
```

print(keyword.iskeyword('Python'))

a. True
b. keyword
c. for
d. False

457.   What will be the output after the following statements?

```
import random
x = [3, 8, 6, 5, 0]
print(random.choice(x))
```

a. A random element from the list x
b. The list x
c. A random element from the list x, excluding 3 and 0
d. A random element from the list elements 3 and 0

458.   What will be the output after the following statements?

```
import random
x = [3, 8, 6, 5, 0]
random.shuffle(x)
print(x)
```

a. A random element from the list x
b. The shuffled list x with the elements mixed up
c. A random element from the list x, excluding 3 and 0
d. A random element from the list elements 3 and 0

459.   What will be the output after the following statements?

```
import random
x = [3, 8, 6, 5, 0]
y = random.shuffle(x)
print(y)
```

a. A random element from the list x
b. The shuffled list x with the elements mixed up
c. None
d. A random element from the list x, excluding 3 and 0

460.   What will be the output after the following statements?

```
import sys
x = sys.stdout.write('Python Jobs')
```

a. A random character from the string 'Python Jobs'
b. Python Jobs
c. None

d. PJ

461.   What will be the output after the following statements?

```
import time
print(time.time())
```

a. Current time in seconds since the Epoch at 00:00:00 GMT on January 1, 1970
b. Today's time in hours
c. None
d. Today's time in minutes

462.   What will be the data type of the output after the following statements?

```
import time
print(time.time())
```

a. String
b. Integer
c. List
d. Float

463.   What will be the data type of the output after the following statements?

```
import time
print(time.asctime())
```

a. String
b. Integer
c. List
d. Float

464.   What will be the output after the following statements?

```
import time
print(time.asctime())
```

a. Current time in seconds since the Epoch at 00:00:00 GMT on January 1, 1970
b. Current date and time
c. None
d. Today's time in minutes

465.   What will be the output after the following statements?

```
import time
y = (2016, 2, 10, 12, 45, 32, 5, 0, 0)
print(time.asctime(y))
```

a. Current time in seconds since the Epoch at 00:00:00 GMT on January 1, 1970
b. Current date and time

c. Sat Feb 10 12:45:32 2016
d. No output

466. What is likely to be the output after the following statements?

```
import time
y = time.asctime()
print(y[:3])
```

a. 2016
b. 3:40
c. Mon
d. 04

467. What will be the output after the following statements?

```
import random
print(int(random.random()*10))
```

a. 10
b. A random integer number within the range of 0 to 9
c. None
d. random floating point number within the range of 0 to 9

468. What will be the output after the following statements?

```
import random
print(int(random.random()*10) + 1)
```

a. 11
b. A random integer number within the range of 0 to 11
c. None
d. A random whole number within the range of 1 to 10

469. What will be the output after the following statements?

```
import random
print(random.sample(range(20), 5))
```

a. A list of 5 unique numbers within the range of 0 to 19
b. A list of 5 unique numbers within the range of 0 to 20
c. A list of 4 unique numbers within the range of 0 to 19
d. A tuple of 5 unique numbers within the range of 0 to 19

470. What will be the output after the following statements?

```
import random
print(random.sample(range(5, 20), 4))
```

a. A list of 5 unique numbers within the range of 4 to 19

b. A list of 5 unique numbers within the range of 5 to 20
c. A list of 4 unique numbers within the range of 5 to 19
d. A tuple of 4 unique numbers within the range of 5 to 19

471.   What will be the output after the following statement?

print(a)

a. SyntaxError
b. TypeError
c. ValueError
d. NameError

472.   What will be the output after the following statement?

a = "Python Practice'

a. SyntaxError
b. TypeError
c. ValueError
d. NameError

473.   What will be the output after the following statement?

a = true

a. No Error
b. TypeError
c. ValueError
d. NameError

474.   What is the value of the NoneType data type?

a. undefined
b. Null
c. Nan
d. None

475.   What will be the output after the following statements?

def xyz():
    a = 56
xyz()
print(a)

a. NameError
b. 56
c. a = 56
d. xyz

476.   What will be the output after the following statements?

```
def xyz():
  x = 40
  abc()
  print(x)
def abc():
  a = 32
  x = 10
xyz()
```

a. NameError
b. 40
c. 10
d. 32

477.   What will be the output after the following statements?

```
def xyz():
  x = 40
def abc():
  xyz()
  a = 32
  x = 10
  print(x)
abc()
```

a. NameError
b. 40
c. 10
d. 32

478.   What will be the output after the following statements?

```
def abc():
  print(x)
x = 10
abc()
```

a. NameError
b. x
c. 10
d. 0

479.   What will be the output after the following statements?

```
def abc():
  x = 12
  print(x)
x = 10
```

```
abc()
```

a. NameError
b. 12
c. 10
d. 0

480.   What will be the output after the following statements?

```
def abc():
    x = 10
    print(x)
abc()
x = 12
```

a. NameError
b. 12
c. 10
d. 0

481.   What will be the output after the following statements?

```
def abc():
    global x
    x = 23
x = 10
abc()
print(x)
```

a. NameError
b. 23
c. 10
d. 0

482.   What will be the output after the following statements?

```
def abc():
    print(x)
    x = 10
abc()
x = 20
```

a. NameError
b. 20
c. 10
d. UnboundLocalError

483.   What will be the output after the following statements?

```
def abc(x):
```

```
    return 20 / x
print(abc(4))
```

a. NameError
b. 5
c. 5.0
d. ZeroDivisionError

484.   What will be the output after the following statements?

```
def abc(x):
    return 20 / x
print(abc(0))
```

a. NameError
b. Undefined
c. 5.0
d. ZeroDivisionError

485.   What will be the output after the following statements?

```
def abc(x):
    try:
        print(20 / x)
    except:
        print('Not a valid argument', end=' ')
print(abc(0))
```

a. NameError
b. Not a valid argument
c. Not a valid argument None
d. ZeroDivisionError

486.   What will be the output after the following statements?

```
def abc(x):
    try:
        print(20 / x)
    except:
        print('Not a valid argument', end=' ')
    finally:
        print(0, end=' ')
print(abc(0))
```

a. Not a valid argument 0 None
b. Not a valid argument
c. Not a valid argument None
d. ZeroDivisionError

487.   What will be the output after the following statements?

```
x = [1, 2, 3, 4]
print(x[4])
```

a. 4
b. 3
c. [1, 2, 3, 4]
d. IndexError

488.   What will be the output after the following statements?

```
x = [10, 20, 30, 40]
print(x[20])
```

a. 20
b. 30
c. [20]
d. IndexError

489.   What will be the output after the following statements?

```
x = [1.0, 2.0, 3.0]
print(x[2.0])
```

a. 2
b. 3.0
c. TypeError
d. IndexError

490.   What will be the output after the following statements?

```
x = [1.0, 2.0, 3.0]
print(x[int(2.0)])
```

a. 2
b. 3.0
c. TypeError
d. IndexError

491.   What will be the output after the following statements?

```
x = ['Today', 'nice', 'day']
print(x[0] + ' is a ' + x[1] + x[2])
```

a. Today is a niceday
b. Today is a nice day
c. Todayis aniceday
d. Todayisaniceday

492.   What will be the output after the following statements?

```
x = ['Today', 'Sunday', 'Monday']
print(x[0] + ' was a great day')
```

a. Today was a great day
b. Sunday was a great day
c. TypeError
d. IndexError

493.   What will be the output after the following statements?

```
x = ['Today', 'Sunday', 'Monday']
print(x[-1] + ' was a great day')
```

a. Today was a great day
b. Sunday was a great day
c. Monday was a great day
d. IndexError

494.   What will be the output after the following statements?

```
x = ['Today', 'Sunday', 'Monday']
print(x[-3] + ' was a great day')
```

a. Today was a great day
b. Sunday was a great day
c. Monday was a great day
d. IndexError

495.   What will be the output after the following statements?

```
x = ['Today', 'Sunday', 'Monday']
x[2] = 'Friday'
x[1] = 'Yesterday'
print(x[-2] + ' was a great day')
```

a. Friday was a great day
b. Sunday was a great day
c. Monday was a great day
d. Yesterday was a great day

496.   What will be the output after the following statements?

```
x = ['Today', 'Sunday', 'Monday']
y = [4, 6, 8]
print(y + x)
```

a. ['Today', 'Sunday', 'Monday', 4, 6, 8]
b. [4, 6, 8, 'Today', 'Sunday', 'Monday']
c. ['Today', 'Sunday', 'Monday']

d. [4, 6, 8]

497.   What will be the output after the following statements?

x = 'Monday'
print('Mon' in x)

a. 'Mon' in x
b. 'Monday' in x
c. True
d. False

498.   What will be the output after the following statements?

x = 'Monday'
print('Day' not in x)

a. 'Day' not in x
b. 'Monday' not in x
c. True
d. False

499.   What will be the output after the following statements?

x = ['hot', '100', True]
weather = x[0]
temperature = x[1]
humid = x[2]
print(weather, temperature, humid)

a. x
b. ['hot', '100', True]
c. 'hot', '100', True
d. hot 100 True

500.   What will be the output after the following statements?

x = ['hot', '100', True]
weather, temperature, humid = x
print(weather, temperature, humid)

a. ValueError
b. ['hot', '100', True]
c. 'hot', '100', True
d. hot 100 True

501.   What will be the output after the following statements?

x = ['hot', '100', True]
weather, humid = x

print(weather, humid)

a. ValueError
b. hot 100
c. hot True
d. hot 100 True

502.   What will be the output after the following statements?

x = ['hot', '100', True]
x.remove('100')
weather, humid = x
print(weather, humid)

a. ValueError
b. hot 100
c. hot True
d. hot 100 True

503.   What will be the output after the following statements?

x = ['a', 'b', 'c', 'A', 'B', 'C']
x.sort()
print(x)

a. SortError
b. ['a', 'b', 'c', 'A', 'B', 'C']
c. ['a', 'A', 'b', 'B', 'c', 'C']
d. ['A', 'B', 'C', 'a', 'b', 'c']

504.   What will be the output after the following statements?

x = ['a', 'b', 'c', 'A', 'B', 'C']
x.sort(key=str.lower)
print(x)

a. SortError
b. ['a', 'b', 'c', 'A', 'B', 'C']
c. ['a', 'A', 'b', 'B', 'c', 'C']
d. ['A', 'B', 'C', 'a', 'b', 'c']

505.   What will be the output after the following statements?

x = ['a', 'b', 'c', 'A', 'B', 'C']
x.sort(key=str.swapcase)
print(x)

a. TypeError
b. ['a', 'b', 'c', 'A', 'B', 'C']
c. ['a', 'A', 'b', 'B', 'c', 'C']

d. ['A', 'B', 'C', 'a', 'b', 'c']

506.   What will be the output after the following statements?

```
x = ['a', 'b', 1, 2, 'A', 'B']
x.sort()
print(x)
```

a. TypeError
b. ['a', 'b', 'c', 'A', 'B', 'C']
c. ['a', 'A', 'b', 'B', 'c', 'C']
d. ['A', 'B', 'C', 'a', 'b', 'c']

507.   What will be the output after the following statements?

```
import random
x = ['Monday', 'Tuesday', 'Wednesday', 'Thursday', 'Friday', 'Saturday', 'Sunday']
print(x[random.randint(0, len(x) - 1)])
```

a. IndexError
b. A random day from all the seven days
c. A random day from all the days except Sunday
d. A random day from all the days except Monday

508.   What will be the output after the following statements?

```
x = 'Today is a nice day' + \
    ' I will go for a walk today'
print(x)
```

a. SyntaxError
b. Today is a nice day
c. I will go for a walk today
d. Today is a nice day I will go for a walk today

509.   What will be the output after the following statements?

```
x = 'Today is a nice day'
x[9] = 'not '
print(x)
```

a. TypeError
b. Today is a nice day
c. SyntaxError
d. Today is not a nice day

510.   What will be the output after the following statements?

```
x = 'Today is a nice day'
y =  x[:9] + 'not ' + x[9:]
```

print(y)

a. TypeError
b. Today is a nice day
c. SyntaxError
d. Today is not a nice day

511.   What will be the output after the following statements?

```
x = 'Today is a nice day'
y =  x[:9] + 'not ' + x[9:]
print(x)
```

a. TypeError
b. Today is a nice day
c. SyntaxError
d. Today is not a nice day

512.   What will be the output after the following statements?

```
x =  'Today is not a nice day'
x = 'Today is a nice day'
print(x)
```

a. TypeError
b. Today is a nice day
c. SyntaxError
d. Today is not a nice day

513.   What will be the output after the following statements?

```
x =  ('Today', 'nice', 'day')
x[1] = 'not'
print(x)
```

a. TypeError
b. ('Today', 'nice', 'day')
c. SyntaxError
d. ('Today', 'not', 'nice', 'day')

514.   What will be the data type of the output after the following statements?

```
x =  ('Today')
print(x)
```

a. TypeError
b. String
c. Tuple
d. List

515.   What will be the data type of the output after the following statements?

x = ('Today',)
print(x)

a. TypeError
b. String
c. Tuple
d. List

516.   What will be the data type of y after the following statements?

x = [1, 2, 3, 4]
y = tuple(x)

a. TypeError
b. String
c. Tuple
d. List

517.   What will be the data type of z after the following statements?

x = [1, 2, 3, 4]
y = tuple(x)
z = list(y)

a. TypeError
b. String
c. Tuple
d. List

518.   What will be the data type of the output after the following statements?

x = 'Python'
y = list(x)
print(y)

a. TypeError
b. String
c. Tuple
d. List

519.   What will be the data type of the output after the following statements?

x = 'Python'
y = tuple(x)
print(y)

a. TypeError
b. String

c. Tuple
d. List

520.   What will be the output after the following statements?

x = ('Python')
print(x)

a. ('P', 'y', 't', 'h', 'o', 'n')
b. Python
c. P y t h o n
d. ('Python')

521.   What will be the output after the following statements?

x = ('Python',)
print(x)

a. ('Python',)
b. Python
c. P y t h o n
d. ('Python')

522.   What will be the output after the following statements?

x = [0, 2, 4, 6]
print(tuple(x))

a. [0, 2, 4, 6]
b. (0, 2, 4, 6)
c. 0, 2, 4, 6
d. 0 2 4 6

523.   What will be the output after the following statements?

x = (0, 2, 4, 6)
print(list(x))

a. [0, 2, 4, 6]
b. (0, 2, 4, 6)
c. 0, 2, 4, 6
d. 0 2 4 6

524.   What will be the output after the following statements?

x = 'Python'
print(list(x))

a. ('P', 'y', 't', 'h', 'o', 'n')
b. (Python)

c. ['P', 'y', 't', 'h', 'o', 'n']
d. ['Python']

525.   What will be the output after the following statements?

```
x = 'Python'
print(tuple(x))
```

a. ('P', 'y', 't', 'h', 'o', 'n')
b. (Python)
c. ['P', 'y', 't', 'h', 'o', 'n']
d. ['Python']

526.   What will be the output after the following statements?

```
x = [4, 5, 7, 8, 9]
y = x
y[1] = 6
print(y)
```

a. [4, 5, 7, 8, 9]
b. [4, 5, 6, 7, 8, 9]
c. [4, 6, 7, 8, 9]
d. [4, 7, 8, 9]

527.   What will be the output after the following statements?

```
x = [4, 5, 7, 8, 9]
y = x
y[1] = 6
print(x)
```

a. [4, 5, 7, 8, 9]
b. [4, 5, 6, 7, 8, 9]
c. [4, 6, 7, 8, 9]
d. [4, 7, 8, 9]

528.   What will be the output after the following statements?

```
def abc(z):
    z.append(44)
x = [7, 8, 9]
abc(x)
print(x)
```

a. [7, 8, 9]
b. [7, 8, 9, 44]
c. [7, 44, 8, 9]
d. [44, 7, 8, 9]

529. What will be the output after the following statements?

```
import copy
x = [5, 4, 3, 2, 1]
y = copy.copy(x)
x.append(6)
print(y[-1])
```

a. 5
b. 6
c. [5, 4, 3, 2, 1, 6]
d. 1

530. What will be the output after the following statements?

```
import copy
x = [5, 4, 3, 2, 1]
y = copy.copy(x)
x[2] = 6
print(y[2])
```

a. 3
b. 6
c. [5, 4, 6, 3, 2, 1]
d. 4

531. What will be the output after the following statements?

```
import copy
x = [5, 4, 3, 2, 1]
y = [7, 8, 9]
z = [x, y]
a = copy.copy(z)
x[2] = 6
print(a)
```

a. [[5, 4, 3, 2, 1], [7, 8, 9]]
b. [[5, 4, 6, 2, 1], [7, 8, 9]]
c. [5, 4, 6, 3, 2, 1]
d. [5, 4, 6, 2, 1, 7, 8, 9]

532. What will be the output after the following statements?

```
import copy
x = [5, 4, 3, 2, 1]
y = [7, 8, 9]
z = [x, y]
a = copy.deepcopy(z)
x[2] = 6
print(a)
```

a. [[5, 4, 3, 2, 1], [7, 8, 9]]
b. [[5, 4, 6, 2, 1], [7, 8, 9]]
c. [5, 4, 6, 3, 2, 1]
d. [5, 4, 6, 2, 1, 7, 8, 9]

533.   What will be the output after the following statements?

```
x = {'day':'Sunday', 'week':10}
print(x['year'])
```

a. day
b. KeyError
c. Sunday
d. 10

534.   What will be the output after the following statements?

```
x = {'day':'Sunday', 'week':10}
for i in x.values():
    print(i, end=' ')
```

a. Sunday 10
b. KeyError
c. Sunday
d. 10

535.   What will be the output after the following statements?

```
x = {'day':'Sunday', 'week':10}
for i in x:
    print(i, end=' ')
```

a. Sunday 10
b. day week
c. Sunday
d. 10

536.   What will be the output after the following statements?

```
x = {'day':'Sunday', 'week':10}
for i in x.keys():
    print(i, end=' ')
```

a. Sunday 10
b. day week
c. Sunday
d. 10

537.   What will be the output after the following statements?

```
x = {'day':'Sunday', 'week':10}
for i in x.items():
    print(i, end=' ')
```

a. ('day', 'Sunday') ('week', 10)
b. day week
c. ('week', 10)
d. ('day', 'Sunday')

538.   What will be the output after the following statements?

```
x = {'day':'Sunday', 'week':10}
print(list(x.keys()))
```

a. Sunday 10
b. day week
c. ['day', 'week']
d. (day, week)

539.   What will be the output after the following statements?

```
x = {'day':'Sunday', 'week':10}
print(tuple(x.items()))
```

a. (('week', 10), ('day', 'Sunday'))
b. ('day', 'Sunday') ('week', 10)
c. ['day', 'week']
d. (day, week)

540.   What will be the output after the following statements?

```
x = {'day':'Sunday', 'week':10}
print(tuple(x.values()))
```

a. Sunday 10
b. ('Sunday', 10)
c. ['Sunday', 10]
d. 10

541.   What will be the output after the following statements?

```
x = {'day':'Sunday', 'week':10}
for i, j in x.items():
    print(i, j, end=' ')
```

a. ('day', 'Sunday') ('week', 10)
b. {'day':'Sunday', 'week':10}
c. 'day':'Sunday', 'week':10
d. day Sunday week 10

542. What will be the output after the following statements?

```
x = {'day':'Sunday', 'week':10}
print('day' in x.values())
```

a. Sunday
b. True
c. False
d. day

543. What will be the output after the following statements?

```
x = {'day':'Sunday', 'week':10}
print('day' in x.keys())
```

a. Sunday
b. True
c. False
d. day

544. What will be the output after the following statements?

```
x = {'day':'Sunday', 'week':10}
print(x.get('day', 'Friday'))
```

a. Friday
b. True
c. Sunday
d. day

545. What will be the output after the following statements?

```
x = {'day':'Sunday', 'week':10}
print(x.get('days', 'Friday'))
```

a. Friday
b. True
c. Sunday
d. day

546. What will be the output after the following statements?

```
x = {'day':'Sunday', 'week':10}
print(x.get('weak', 5))
```

a. 10
b. 5
c. Sunday
d. day

547.   What will be the output after the following statements?

```
x = {'day':'Sunday', 'week':10}
print(x.get('week', 5))
```

    a. 10
    b. 5
    c. Sunday
    d. day

548.   What will be the output after the following statements?

```
x = {'day':'Sunday', 'week':10}
print(x.get('year', 2016))
```

    a. year
    b. 2016
    c. Sunday
    d. 10

549.   What will be the output after the following statements?

```
x = {'year': 2016, 'month': 'March'}
if 'day' not in x:
    x['day'] = 'Tuesday'
print(x)
```

    a. ('day', 'Tuesday')
    b. {'day': 'Tuesday', 'month': 'March'}
    c. 'day': 'Tuesday', 'month': 'March', 'year': 2016
    d. {'day': 'Tuesday', 'month': 'March', 'year': 2016}

550.   What will be the output after the following statements?

```
x = {'year': 2016, 'month': 'March'}
x.setdefault('day', 'Tuesday')
print(x)
```

    a. ('day', 'Tuesday')
    b. {'day': 'Tuesday', 'month': 'March'}
    c. 'day': 'Tuesday', 'month': 'March', 'year': 2016
    d. {'day': 'Tuesday', 'month': 'March', 'year': 2016}

551.   What will be the output after the following statements?

```
x = {'year': 2016, 'month': 'March'}
x.setdefault('day', 'Tuesday')
x.setdefault('day', 'Monday')
print(x)
```

a. ('day', 'Monday')
b. {'day': 'Monday', 'month': 'March'}
c. {'day': 'Tuesday', 'month': 'March', 'year': 2016}
da. {'day': 'Monday', 'month': 'March', 'year': 2016}

552.   What will be the data type of x after the following statement?

x = {}

a. Tuple
b. Set
c. List
d. Dictionary

553.   What will be the output after the following statement?

print(r'Today is a \n nice day')

a. Today is a \n nice day
b. Today is a
   nice day
c. Today is a nice day
d. 'Today is a \n nice day'

554.   What will be the output after the following statements?

x = 'python jobs'
x.upper()
print(x)

a. PYTHON JOBS
b. Python jobs
c. Python Jobs
d. python jobs

555.   What will be the output after the following statements?

x = 'Python Jobs'
x.lower()
print(x)

a. PYTHON JOBS
b. Python jobs
c. Python Jobs
d. python jobs

556.   What will be the output after the following statements?

x = 'Python Jobs'

```
if x.lower() == 'python jobs':
    print('Python jobs')
else:
    print('python 3 jobs')
```

a. python 3 jobs
b. Python jobs
c. Python Jobs
d. python jobs

557.   What will be the output after the following statements?

```
x = 'Python Jobs'
if x.isupper():
    print('Python jobs')
else:
    print('python 3 jobs')
```

a. python 3 jobs
b. Python jobs
c. Python Jobs
d. python jobs

558.   What will be the output after the following statements?

```
x = 'Python Jobs'
y = x.upper().lower().upper()
print(y)
```

a. python Jobs
b. PYTHON JOBS
c. Python Jobs
d. python jobs

559.   What will be the output after the following statements?

```
x = 'Python Jobs'
y = x.upper().lower().isupper()
print(y)
```

a. python jobs
b. PYTHON JOBS
c. False
d. True

560.   What will be the output after the following statements?

```
x = ['Python', 'is', 'interesting']
y = ' '.join(x)
print(y)
```

a. 'Python', 'is', 'interesting'
b. Python is interesting
c. Pythonisinteresting
d. ['Python', 'is', 'interesting']

561.   What will be the output after the following statements?

```
x = 'Python is interesting'
y = x.split()
print(y)
```

a. 'Python', 'is', 'interesting'
b. Python is interesting
c. Pythonisinteresting
d. ['Python', 'is', 'interesting']

562.   What will be the output after the following statements?

```
x = '''Today is a nice day.
Let's go for a walk.
We'll also go to the park.'''
y = x.split('\n')
print(y)
```

a. ['Today is a nice day.', "Let's go for a walk.", "We'll also go to the park."]
b. Today is a nice day.
c. Let's go for a walk.
d. We'll also go to the park.

563.   What will be the output after the following statements?

```
x = 'Python 2 and Python 3'
print(x.strip('and'))
```

a. Python 2
b. Python 3
c. Python 2 and Python 3
d. Python 2 Python 3

564.   What will be the output after the following statements?

```
x = 'Python 2 and Python 3'
print(x.strip('thon 3'))
```

a. Python 2
b. Python 2 and Py
c. Python 2 and Python 3
d. Python 2 Python 3

565.   What is the first line of the following statements on Windows?

```
#! python3
x = 'Python 3'
```

a. A comment
b. Python String
c. Shebang line
d. Python Variable

566.   What will be the output after the following statements?

```
import re
x = re.compile(r'\d\d\d-\d\d\d\d')
y = x.search('The phone number is 444-4444')
print(y.group())
```

a. The phone number is 444-4444
b. \d\d\d-\d\d\d\d
c. 444-4444
d. r'\d\d\d-\d\d\d\d'

567.   What will be the output after the following statements?

```
import re
x = re.compile(r'(\d\d\d)-(\d\d\d\d)')
y = x.search('The phone number is 444-4444')
print(y.group(2))
```

a. The phone number is 444-4444
b. 4444
c. 444-4444
d. 444

568.   What will be the output after the following statements?

```
import re
x = re.compile(r'(\d\d\d)-(\d\d\d\d)')
y = x.search('The phone number is 444-4444')
print(y.group(1))
```

a. The phone number is 444-4444
b. 4444
c. 444-4444
d. 444

569.   What will be the output after the following statements?

```
import re
x = re.compile(r'(\d\d\d)-(\d\d\d\d)')
```

```
y = x.search('The phone number is 444-4444')
print(y.group(0))
```

a. The phone number is 444-4444
b. 4444
c. 444-4444
d. 444

570.   What will be the output after the following statements?

```
import re
x = re.compile(r'(\d\d\d)-(\d\d\d\d)')
y = x.search('The phone number is 444-4444')
print(y.groups())
```

a. ('444', '4444')
b. 4444
c. 444-4444
d. 444

571.   What will be the output after the following statements?

```
import re
x = re.compile(r'(\(\d\d\d\))-(\d\d\d\d)')
y = x.search('The phone number is (444)-4444')
print(y.group(1))
```

a. ('444', '4444')
b. 444
c. 444-4444
d. (444)

572.   What will be the output after the following statements?

```
import re
x = re.compile(r'Python 2|Python 3')
y = x.search('Python 3 MCQ')
print(y.group())
```

a. Python 2|Python 3
b. Python 2
c. Python 3
d. Python 3 MCQ

573.   What will be the output after the following statements?

```
import re
x = re.compile(r'Python 2|Python 3')
y = x.search('Python 2.7')
print(y.group())
```

a. Python 2.7
b. Python 2
c. Python 3
d. Python 2|Python 3

574.   What will be the output after the following statements?

```
import re
x = re.compile(r'day')
y = x.search('Today is a nice day and a Sunday')
print(y.group())
```

a. day
b. Today
c. nice day
d. Sunday

575.   What will be the output after the following statements?

```
import re
x = re.compile(r'(Sun)?day')
y = x.search('Today is a nice day and a Sunday')
print(y.group())
```

a. day
b. Today
c. nice day
d. Sunday

576.   What will be the output after the following statements?

```
import re
x = re.compile(r'(Sun|To)?day')
y = x.search('Today is a nice day and a Sunday')
print(y.group())
```

a. day
b. Today
c. nice day
d. Sunday

577.   What will be the output after the following statements?

```
import re
x = re.compile(r'(Sun)*day')
y = x.search('Today is a nice day and a Sunday')
print(y.group())
```

a. nice day

b. Today
c. day
d. Sunday

578.   What will be the output after the following statements?

```
import re
x = re.compile(r'(Sun)+day')
y = x.search('Today is a nice day and a Sunday')
print(y.group())
```

a. day
b. Today
c. nice day
d. Sunday

579.   What will be the output after the following statements?

```
import re
x = re.compile(r'(Python){2}')
y = x.search('PythonPythonPython')
print(y.group())
```

a. PythonPythonPython
b. PythonPython
c. Python
d. Python 2

580.   What will be the output after the following statements?

```
import re
x = re.compile(r'(Python){2,3}')
y = x.search('PythonPythonPython')
print(y.group())
```

a. PythonPythonPython
b. PythonPython
c. Python
d. Python 2

581.   What will be the output after the following statements?

```
import re
x = re.compile(r'(Python){1,3}?')
y = x.search('PythonPythonPython')
print(y.group())
```

a. PythonPythonPython
b. PythonPython
c. Python

d. Python 2

582.   What will be the output after the following statements?

```
import re
x = re.compile(r'day')
y = x.findall('Today is a nice day and a Sunday')
print(y)
```

a. day
b. Today
c. ['day', 'day', 'day']
d. ('day', 'day', 'day')

583.   What will be the output after the following statements?

```
import re
x = re.compile(r'(Sun)?day')
y = x.findall('Today is a nice day and a Sunday')
print(y)
```

a. ('day', 'day', 'day')
b. ['', '', 'Sun']
c. ['day', 'day', 'day']
d. Sunday

584.   What will be the output after the following statements?

```
import re
x = re.compile(r'(Sun|To)?day')
y = x.findall('Today is a nice day and a Sunday')
print(y)
```

a. ('day', 'day', 'day')
b. ['', '', 'Sun']
c. ['day', 'day', 'day']
d. ['To', '', 'Sun']

585.   What will be the output after the following statements?

```
import re
x = re.compile(r'(Sun)*day')
y = x.findall('Today is a nice day and a Sunday')
print(y)
```

a. ('day', 'day', 'day')
b. ['', '', 'Sun']
c. ['day', 'day', 'day']
d. ['To', '', 'Sun']

586. What will be the output after the following statements?

```
import re
x = re.compile(r'(Sun)+day')
y = x.findall('Today is a nice day and a Sunday')
print(y)
```

a. ['', '', 'Sun']
b. ['Sun']
c. ['day', 'day', 'day']
d. ['To', '', 'Sun']

587. What will be the output after the following statements?

```
import re
x = re.compile(r'(\(\d\d\d\))-(\d\d\d\d)')
y = x.findall('The phone number is (444)-4444')
print(y)
```

a. [('(444)', '4444')]
b. [('444)', '4444']
c. (('(444)', '4444'))
d. ('444', '4444')

588. What will be the output after the following statements?

```
import re
x = re.compile(r'\d')
y = x.findall('The phone number is (444)-4444')
print(y)
```

a. [('(444)', '4444')]
b. '4', '4', '4', '4', '4', '4', '4'
c. (('(444)', '4444'))
d. ['4', '4', '4', '4', '4', '4', '4']

589. What will be the output after the following statements?

```
import re
x = re.compile(r'\D')
y = x.findall('Python 3')
print(y)
```

a. ['Python', '3']
b. ['P', 'y', 't', 'h', 'o', 'n', ' ', '3']
c. ['P', 'y', 't', 'h', 'o', 'n', ' ']
d. ['P', 'y', 't', 'h', 'o', 'n']

590. What will be the output after the following statements?

```
import re
x = re.compile(r'\w')
y = x.findall('Python_3')
print(y)
```

   a. ['Python', '3']
   b. ['P', 'y', 't', 'h', 'o', 'n', '3']
   c. ['P', 'y', 't', 'h', 'o', 'n', ' ']
   d. ['P', 'y', 't', 'h', 'o', 'n', '_', '3']

591.   What will be the output after the following statements?

```
import re
x = re.compile(r'\W')
y = x.findall('Python_3')
print(y)
```

   a. ['Python', '3']
   b. []
   c. ['P', 'y', 't', 'h', 'o', 'n', ' ']
   d. [' ']

592.   What will be the output after the following statements?

```
import re
x = re.compile(r'\s')
y = x.findall('Python 3')
print(y)
```

   a. ['Python', '3']
   b. []
   c. ['P', 'y', 't', 'h', 'o', 'n', ' ']
   d. [' ']

593.   What will be the output after the following statements?

```
import re
x = re.compile(r'\S')
y = x.findall('Python 3')
print(y)
```

   a. ['P', 'y', 't', 'h', 'o', 'n', '3']
   b. []
   c. ['P', 'y', 't', 'h', 'o', 'n', ' ']
   d. [' ']

594.   What will be the output after the following statements?

```
import re
x = re.compile(r'[0-9]')
```

```
y = x.findall('Python 3')
print(y)
```

a. ['P', 'y', 't', 'h', 'o', 'n', '3']
b. []
c. ['3']
d. [' ']

595.   What will be the output after the following statements?

```
import re
x = re.compile(r'[ptPT]')
y = x.findall('Python 3')
print(y)
```

a. ['P', 't', 'h', 'o', 'n']
b. ['P', 't']
c. []
d. [' ']

596.   What will be the output after the following statements?

```
import re
x = re.compile(r'[p-t0-6]')
y = x.findall('Python 3')
print(y)
```

a. ['P', 't', '3']
b. ['P', 't']
c. []
d. ['t', '3']

597.   What will be the output after the following statements?

```
import re
x = re.compile(r'[D-S0-2]')
y = x.findall('Python 3')
print(y)
```

a. ['P', 't', '3']
b. ['P', 't']
c. ['P']
d. ['t', '3']

598.   What will be the output after the following statements?

```
import re
x = re.compile(r'[^A-Za-z0-2]')
y = x.findall('Python_3')
print(y)
```

a. ['_', '3']
b. ['P', 't']
c. [' ', '3']
d. ['t', '3']

599.   What will be the output after the following statements?

```
import re
x = re.compile(r'^Py')
y = x.search('Python_3')
print(y.group())
```

a. ['Py']
b. Py
c. ['P', 'y']
d. ['P', 'y', '3']

600.   What will be the output after the following statements?

```
import re
x = re.compile(r'3$')
print(x.search('Python_3') == None)
```

a. ['3']
b. Python_3
c. True
d. False

601.   What will be the output after the following statements?

```
import re
x = re.compile(r'.day')
y = x.findall('Today is a nice day and a Sunday')
print(y)
```

a. ['oday', 'nday']
b. ['oday', ' day', 'nday']
c. ['day', 'day', 'day']
d. ['Today', ' day', 'Sunday']

602.   What will be the output after the following statements?

```
import re
x = re.compile(r'(.*)day')
y = x.findall('Today is a nice day and a Sunday')
print(y)
```

a. ['To']
ba. ['Today is a nice day and a Sunday']

c. ['Today is a nice day and a Sun']
d. ['Today is a nice day']

603.   What will be the output after the following statements?

```
import re
x = re.compile(r'(.*?)day')
y = x.findall('Today is a nice day and a Sunday')
print(y)
```

a. ['To', ' is a nice ', ' and a Sun']
b. ['Today is a nice day and a Sunday']
c. ['Today is a nice day and a Sun']
d. ['Today is a nice day']

604.   What will be the output after the following statements?

```
import re
x = re.compile('.*')
y = x.search("Today is a nice day.\n Let's go for a walk.\n We'll also go to the park.")
print(y.group())
```

a. Today is a nice day.\n Let's go for a walk.\n We'll also go to the park.
b. Today is a nice day.\n Let's go for a walk.
c. ['Today is a nice day.']
d. Today is a nice day.

605.   What will be the output after the following statements?

```
import re
x = re.compile('.*', re.DOTALL)
y = x.search("Today is a nice day.\n Let's go for a walk.\n We'll also go to the park.")
print(y.group())
```

a. Today is a nice day.
Let's go for a walk.
We'll also go to the park.
b. Today is a nice day.\n Let's go for a walk.
c. ['Today is a nice day.']
d. Today is a nice day.

606.   What will be the output after the following statements?

```
import re
x = re.compile('Day')
y = x.search('Today is a nice day')
print(y)
```

a. Today is a nice day.
b. None

c. ['Today is a nice day.']
d. (Today is a nice day.)

607.   What will be the output after the following statements?

```
import re
x = re.compile('Day', re.I)
y = x.search('Today is a nice day')
print(y.group())
```

a. Today is a nice day.
b. None
c. ['Today is a nice day.']
d. day

608.   What will be the output after the following statements?

```
import re
x = re.compile('day', re.IGNORECASE)
y = x.findall('Today is a nice day and a Sunday')
print(y)
```

a. [Today is a nice day.]
b. ['day', 'day']
c. ['day', 'day', 'day']
d. day

609.   What will be the output after the following statements?

```
import re
x = re.compile('Sunday')
y = x.sub('Wednesday', 'Today is a nice day and a Sunday')
print(y)
```

a. Today is a nice day
b. Today is a nice day and a Sunday
c. ['Sunday']
d. Today is a nice day and a Wednesday

610.   What will be the output after the following statements?

```
import os
x = os.getcwd()
print(x)
```

a. Name of the operating system
b. Version of the operating system
c. The current working directory
d. Name of the current file

611.   What do the following statements do?

import webbrowser
webbrowser.open('http://google.com')

a. Ping http://google.com
b. Display http://google.com in the shell
c. Download http://google.com as a text file
d. Launch a browser window to http://google.com

612.   What will be the output after the following statements?

import sys
print(sys.argv)

a. A set of the program's filename and command line arguments
b. A list of the program's filename and command line arguments
c. A tuple of the program's filename and command line arguments
d. A dictionary of the program's filename and command line arguments

Answer Key

1. b
2. c
3. c
4. b
5. a
6. d
7. b
8. d
9. c
10. b
11. b
12. a
13. d
14. c
15. b
16. c
17. a
18. a
19. b
20. d
21. c
22. d
23. a
24. c
25. d
26. b
27. a
28. b
29. b
30. a
31. b
32. a
33. d
34. c
35. c
36. d
37. b
38. a

S.C. Lewis

39. b
40. c
41. b
42. d
43. a
44. b
45. b
46. c
47. c
48. a
49. a
50. c
51. b
52. d
53. a
54. d
55. c
56. d
57. c
58. a
59. d
60. b
61. b
62. c
63. a
64. d
65. a
66. d
67. b
68. d
69. a
70. c
71. b
72. b
73. c
74. d
75. a
76. b
77. a
78. d
79. a
80. c

S.C. Lewis

81. b
82. d
83. b
84. a
85. c
86. b
87. a
88. d
89. b
90. c
91. d
92. c
93. c
94. d
95. b
96. c
97. d
98. a
99. a
100. b
101. c
102. d
103. b
104. a
105. c
106. a
107. b
108. d
109. d
110. d
111. a
112. b
113. c
114. b
115. d
116. a
117. c
118. c
119. d
120. b
121. b
122. a

123. d
124. a
125. c
126. b
127. a
128. d
129. b
130. a
131. d
132. b
133. c
134. b
135. d
136. c
137. a
138. d
139. b
140. b
141. c
142. d
143. a
144. b
145. c
146. a
147. b
148. a
149. b
150. c
151. d
152. a
153. c
154. b
155. a
156. d
157. b
158. c
159. a
160. c
161. c
162. d
163. b
164. d

165. a
166. d
167. b
168. a
169. d
170. c
171. a
172. b
173. d
174. a
175. c
176. d
177. a
178. c
179. b
180. a
181. b
182. c
183. d
184. a
185. c
186. b
187. d
188. b
189. c
190. a
191. b
192. a
193. c
194. c
195. d
196. b
197. a
198. b
199. d
200. c
201. d
202. c
203. a
204. a
205. b
206. d

207. c
208. b
209. a
210. b
211. d
212. c
213. d
214. b
215. c
216. d
217. c
218. a
219. b
220. d
221. c
222. b
223. d
224. a
225. c
226. a
227. d
228. b
229. b
230. a
231. a
232. c
233. b
234. d
235. a
236. c
237. b
238. a
239. a
240. b
241. d
242. c
243. c
244. d
245. d
246. b
247. b
248. a

249. a
250. a
251. b
252. c
253. a
254. b
255. a
256. b
257. d
258. d
259. a
260. b
261. c
262. d
263. d
264. c
265. d
266. c
267. c
268. d
269. c
270. d
271. d
272. c
273. a
274. b
275. a
276. b
277. b
278. a
279. c
280. a
281. b
282. d
283. c
284. b
285. a
286. d
287. b
288. d
289. b
290. a

291. c
292. a
293. c
294. b
295. a
296. b
297. d
298. c
299. b
300. a
301. c
302. a
303. b
304. d
305. b
306. d
307. b
308. d
309. c
310. c
311. a
312. d
313. b
314. d
315. b
316. c
317. c
318. b
319. a
320. a
321. d
322. c
323. a
324. b
325. d
326. b
327. c
328. a
329. b
330. d
331. b
332. a

333. c
334. d
335. a
336. c
337. b
338. a
339. d
340. a
341. b
342. c
343. d
344. a
345. b
346. c
347. a
348. b
349. d
350. a
351. b
352. d
353. c
354. a
355. d
356. c
357. b
358. b
359. a
360. d
361. c
362. b
363. d
364. d
365. a
366. b
367. c
368. b
369. d
370. c
371. a
372. b
373. d
374. c

375. c
376. b
377. b
378. d
379. c
380. d
381. a
382. b
383. c
384. d
385. d
386. a
387. b
388. c
389. d
390. a
391. b
392. c
393. b
394. b
395. b
396. d
397. b
398. c
399. a
400. a
401. b
402. a
403. a
404. d
405. c
406. c
407. b
408. d
409. c
410. b
411. d
412. c
413. b
414. a
415. d
416. b

417. c
418. c
419. a
420. c
421. d
422. b
423. d
424. b
425. c
426. a
427. c
428. b
429. d
430. a
431. d
432. c
433. d
434. c
435. b
436. c
437. b
438. a
439. b
440. a
441. c
442. c
443. b
444. d
445. b
446. d
447. c
448. d
449. c
450. b
451. a
452. c
453. d
454. d
455. a
456. d
457. a
458. b

459. c
460. b
461. a
462. d
463. a
464. b
465. c
466. c
467. b
468. d
469. a
470. c
471. d
472. a
473. d
474. d
475. a
476. b
477. c
478. c
479. b
480. c
481. b
482. d
483. c
484. d
485. c
486. a
487. d
488. d
489. c
490. b
491. a
492. a
493. c
494. a
495. d
496. b
497. c
498. c
499. d
500. d

501. a
502. c
503. d
504. c
505. b
506. a
507. b
508. d
509. a
510. d
511. b
512. b
513. a
514. b
515. c
516. c
517. d
518. d
519. c
520. b
521. a
522. b
523. a
524. c
525. a
526. c
527. c
528. b
529. d
530. a
531. b
532. a
533. b
534. a
535. b
536. b
537. a
538. c
539. a
540. b
541. d
542. c

543. b
544. c
545. a
546. b
547. a
548. b
549. d
550. d
551. c
552. d
553. a
554. d
555. c
556. b
557. a
558. b
559. c
560. b
561. d
562. a
563. c
564. b
565. c
566. c
567. b
568. d
569. c
570. a
571. d
572. c
573. b
574. a
575. a
576. b
577. c
578. d
579. b
580. a
581. c
582. c
583. b
584. d

585. b
586. b
587. a
588. d
589. c
590. d
591. b
592. d
593. a
594. c
595. b
596. d
597. c
598. a
599. b
600. d
601. b
602. c
603. a
604. d
605. a
606. b
607. d
608. c
609. d
610. c
611. d
612. b

Thank You

Thanks for buying this book. If you find an errors or have any suggestions, feel free to let me know at sclewis2016@outlook.com

---

More Books by the Author

If you liked this book, you might want to check the other books by the author too.

Python 3 MCQ - Multiple Choice Questions n Answers for Tests, Quizzes - Python Students & Teachers

Python3 101 MCQ - Multiple Choice Questions Answers for Jobs, Tests and Quizzes

www.ingramcontent.com/pod-product-compliance
Lightning Source LLC
Chambersburg PA
CBHW080420060326
40689CB00019B/4317